A
POCKET GUIDE
TO
SUSTAINABLE FOOD SHOPPING

A POCKET GUIDE

TO

SUSTAINABLE FOOD SHOPPING

HOW TO NAVIGATE THE GROCERY STORE, READ LABELS, AND HELP SAVE THE PLANET

Kate Bratskeir

TILLER PRESS

New York   London   Toronto   Sydney   New Delhi

TILLER PRESS

An Imprint of Simon & Schuster, Inc.
1230 Avenue of the Americas
New York, NY 10020

First Tiller Press trade paperback edition January 2021

TILLER PRESS and colophon are trademarks of Simon & Schuster, Inc.

For information about special discounts for bulk purchases, please contact
Simon & Schuster Special Sales at 1-866-506-1949
or business@simonandschuster.com.

The Simon & Schuster Speakers Bureau can bring authors to your live event.
For more information or to book an event, contact the Simon & Schuster Speakers
Bureau at 1-866-248-3049 or visit our website at www.simonspeakers.com.

Interior design by Laura Levatino

Manufactured in the United States of America

1   3   5   7   9   10   8   6   4   2

Library of Congress Cataloging-in-Publication Data

Names: Bratskeir, Kate, author.
Title: A pocket guide to sustainable food shopping : how to navigate the grocery
store, read labels, and help save the planet / by Kate Bratskeir.
Description: First Tiller Press trade paperback edition. | New York : Tiller Press, 2020. |
Includes bibliographical references and index.
Identifiers: LCCN 2020016363 (print) | LCCN 2020016364 (ebook) | ISBN
9781982150068 (paperback) | ISBN 9781982150075 (ebook)
Subjects: LCSH: Grocery shopping. | Nutrition.
Classification: LCC TX356 .B73 2020 (print) | LCC TX356 (ebook) | DDC 641.3/1—dc23
LC record available at https://lccn.loc.gov/2020016363
LC ebook record available at https://lccn.loc.gov/2020016364

ISBN 978-1-9821-5006-8
ISBN 978-1-9821-5007-5 (ebook)

To Ben, for being the best

CONTENTS

Contents

A POCKET GUIDE TO

SUSTAINABLE FOOD SHOPPING

INTRODUCTION

*T*here are some things you should know.

First, I'm so glad you're here. I'm excited by this growing, collective desire to make changes to become more sustainable so our planet can thrive. Maybe you've seen the images of plastic-covered seashores, animals with their heads caught in milk jugs, and countries engulfed in so much food packaging, the debris makes mountains of its own. You've read headlines about rising temperatures, melting ice caps, raging fires. Maybe you know that the people responsible for growing the food we eat are those most likely to go hungry. Or that our obsession with almond milk is sabotaging the bee population. **Whatever you know, you also know you want to do something about it.**

The good news is that there's a lot you can do. And I hope these pages can serve as your guidebook for making an impact. Feel free to jump around these pages and focus on the chapters that matter to you. From cutting down on your food and packaging waste to knowing what to look for in so-called sustainable seafood, you'll learn how to form buying (and not-buying!) decisions that do more good than harm.

But the truth is, even if you resolve to use a tote bag at the supermarket for eternity and follow the rest of these to-dos, you will by no means save the world. I believe there's a lot of good service in this book, and if you want to, you can learn a lot. Still, it's not enough.

SO WHY BOTHER?

It can feel so futile—hopeless?—to change a habit, knowing every little adjustment is just a tiny drop in a bucket. But what you do will have an impact as it echoes among your family, your community, your grocery store, your favorite oat milk brand, and the food industry at large. The food system is deeply flawed, and systemic change needs to come from the inside if we're going to combat climate change, feed more people, treat both laborers and animals with humanity, and continue to share in the joy of food. The food industry, however, is going to stay exactly the same if, by surrendering with inaction, we allow it to.

The fact that just 9 percent of the world's plastic is recycled, and that most of the remaining 91 percent leaches toxins into our waterways and threatens the livelihoods of people, animals, and ecosystems, and that all this junk will outlive us—this is not your fault.[1] Corporations and retailers both have a role to play in our giant plastic problem, and as consumers, our role is to communicate that we no longer stand for it. We can do that by writing our own rules and spending our money with those who want to take responsibility and get this right.

Throughout the process of writing this book, I've struggled a lot with guilt. I've read so much that emphasizes how the world is on fire, and here I am, trying to extinguish the flames by telling people how to buy rice from the bulk section of the supermarket. The scale seems severely imbalanced here.

My defense, as I do my best to reconcile, is this: I've collected some information that I've thoroughly researched, I've put time into these pages, and maybe I can teach someone something new. Maybe this book will serve as a gateway to real, productive change. Maybe if enough of us carve out portals that motivate people and their communities to make positive change, the needle will move with us.

I'm trying. Your reading this book means that you're trying, too. The only thing I know is that this has to be better than not trying at all.

1.

ENVIRONMENTAL GUILT SYNDROME

Once you begin to notice plastic and other needless waste, you won't be able to stop noticing. You'll wonder why that tin of organic nuts you bought had to come with a plastic seal. You'll roll your eyes at plastic straws, kick yourself for allowing a beautiful bunch of carrots to shrivel, feel physically ill over taking a swig from a plastic water bottle, and question why the hell you have so many Christmas ornaments, anyway.

I've spent a lot of time feeling really terrible about every imperfect purchasing decision I've made. (Sometimes I can't bear to tell a cashier I have my own bag when they've already expertly packed my stuff.) Anne Marie Bonneau, aka the Zero-Waste Chef, has dubbed this condition Environmental Guilt Syndrome. EGS stems from the desire to be perfect in the decisions you make to cut your plastic consumption and never let a sweet potato sprout eyes and wrinkle again. But "it's impossible to be perfect," Bonneau says. "I think if you try to be perfect, you're just going to be paralyzed, and you might not do anything."

Bonneau's EGS is along the same lines as "eco-anxiety," a condition the American Psychological Association describes as the feelings of helplessness and dread associated with "watching the slow and seemingly irrevocable impacts of climate change unfold, and worrying about the future for oneself, children, and later generations."[1] This is real stuff.

There's a saying that's popular in the waste-focused space that might help you shake some guilt: "We don't need a handful of people doing zero waste perfectly. We need millions of people doing it imperfectly."

Also: the gargantuan amount of waste our world has produced, collected, and improperly disposed of—none of that is your fault. "Our society is not set up to make it easy to live sustainably," Bonneau points out. "We're all swimming upstream."

But the point is we're still swimming. More and more people are committing to sustainable practices every day, and for this reason, we can have hope.

I ask you to find solace in the fact that you will never be perfect (in your fight against food waste—or anything, really).

Accepting this imperfection will free you to make progress.

2.

HOW TO START
(BEING LESS OF A GARBAGE PERSON)

Start small.

Practicing sustainable food shopping and consumption isn't going to happen in a day because there's a lot to change. If you don't know where to begin, first know that you're not alone. Anne Marie Bonneau says that "How do I start?" is the most common question she gets from her readers, and she always advises starting with something small.

Maybe you kick things off with a **waste audit**, which is when you observe and track your trash for a week to see what's taking up the most space. Let's say you notice a bottle of a certain beverage is crowding your trash can. Can you stop buying this product? If it's something you're unwilling to live without, can you make your own version at home or find an alternative that can be purchased in a reusable container? Make one of these choices, and you've done it—you're one step closer to living "zero waste." Now that you've gotten rid of this hypothetical bottle, pick the next most common item in your waste bin to remove or replace.

In the back of this book you'll find some blank, lined pages that you can fill out to do your own waste audit at home. This is me asking you to dig through your garbage. The pages are set up to provide you with a way to see all your waste at once, and take action from there.

This is really important: while you go through this process of reducing your consumption of planet-harming products, don't forget to recognize your progress. It's easy to focus on what you're *not* doing, or what you *could* be doing better, but this just lowers your self-esteem and worsens your EGS. Celebrate the changes you've successfully made; when positive reinforcement is part of the equation, you're more likely to stick to a new behavior.[1] So be nice to yourself.

Also, however you start, and whatever you're finding works, make sure you **talk about it**. You don't have preach, but you can share the positive changes you've made in your own life with your community, and the changes you'd like to see with shop owners, manufacturers, and people in power. Bonneau says this is how grassroots movements start. The Break Free From Plastic Pollution Act of 2020 (HR 5845)—which would've required producers to take responsibility for collecting and recycling materials associated with their products if it had passed—probably wouldn't have reached Congress if people hadn't complained about the dumb, excessive packaging that comes with their food.[2]

Shilpi Chhotray, senior communications officer for Break Free From Plastic, says kvetching about plastic waste is how change will come (okay, she didn't say kvetching). "The bigger-picture change is going to happen at the corporate level," she says, adding that writing to corporations, "tagging them on social media, and demanding they change their practices and move to systems of refill and reuse" are ways we can incite corporate-level change. Chhotray says **social media shaming can be effective**, since public complaints are so visible and often gain viral support. (There's also benefit in using your social media platforms for good, sharing your praise for companies that are working to get it right.)

Another behavior that can help reduce your waste? **Cook more meals at home.** "If you know how to cook, you won't waste food," Bonneau says. And, she adds, you don't have to cook up anything fancy (unless you want to, which, by all means, go for it). When you shop for ingredients at the grocery store or farmers' market, choose ones that come in little to no packaging (more on this ahead). Google some "one pot" or "zero waste" recipes, and you'll see that the internet is a gift.

When you start cooking more, try your best to **abandon any preconceived notion of what a "meal" means.** Both food brands and industries have executed stellar marketing to ensure that you believe breakfast, lunch, and dinner must include a hunk of meat with sides in order to constitute a meal. This marketing has been so effective that you might be psychologically conditioned to believe you feel hungry unless you've had a "proper" meal.

Brooks Headley, owner of the tiny, all-vegetarian restaurant Superiority Burger in Manhattan, told *GQ* that he's seen this dilemma come up with his customers. "Sometimes people are like, 'Well then, what am I, just eating sides?' They're like, 'It's just a bunch of sides!' To which I say, 'Yeah, so what!' . . . Everything you eat doesn't have to be like a chunk of protein and a pile of vegetables."[3]

In other words, you don't have to cook a roast to make yourself a meal; you could actually just whip up a bunch of vegetables in a tasty way that you love and call it dinner. If you're really struggling to wrap your head around this, maybe your new mantra needs to be "Sides can be a meal."

Say it three times in the mirror every morning when you wake up—really look yourself in the eye when you do it—and three times again as you chop up some broccoli to pair with leftover quinoa for dinner. Soon enough, you'll have overcome the misleading, imprisoning, socially imposed paradigm that's kept you from cooking differently for all these years.

Taking home less waste, in some cases, may have to **start by asking for it.** Ask for your deli cheese and meats to be placed in containers you bring from home. Ask for your leftovers to be stored in the spare mason jars you carry with you to restaurants. Ask for your cocktail to come without a straw. There's no harm in asking.

Finally, you might also wear your desire to reduce your carbon footprint on your sleeve (or shoulder). If you haven't already, **commit to taking your own bag** to the grocery store once and for all.

As more counties, states, and countries continue to ban plastic bags, it'll become increasingly important to take your own bag to the supermarket. No matter how many sweet totes you have collected in a corner of a closet, the act of actually taking a few to the store is the most crucial step. A UK study found that a single cotton tote bag has to be used 131 times before it has less global warming potential than a single-use plastic bag.[4] So you're definitely better off using the tote bags you already have, rather than buying new cotton bags stamped with an inspiring quote or an adorable pug illustration to launch your environmental journey.

Apply this same concept to produce and bread bags. Yes, they make little reusable bags for bread and fruit. If this excites you and you think you'll use them at every grocery haul, go get 'em. Still, using materials you already have on hand is probably the more responsible move. For the crafty and patient: Can you repurpose an old T-shirt into a bag with a couple of stitches? If you've used plastic produce bags, can you store them at the bottom of your tote bag to be reused on a future trip?

Paper bags, by the way, won't make your grocery shopping any more virtuous. You may have been taught that paper trumps plastic, but according to research from the Northern Ireland Assembly, a paper bag has to be reused about three times to earn a lower carbon footprint than a plastic one.[5] This is because it takes about four times as much energy to produce a paper bag as it does to make a plastic bag.

Again, remembering to take these materials to the store can be the hardest part. Here's a list of suggestions from people who've done their best to make remembering second nature.

HOW TO REMEMBER TO TAKE A GODDAMN TOTE BAG TO THE GROCERY STORE

- Get a clip-on, foldable bag that you can attach to your keys or your purse.
- Keep some mesh produce bags in your purse so they're accessible, too, if you have room.
- Store bags in your car's trunk so you always have them handy.
- If you don't drive, stash a few bags by the front door so you'll remember to take them with you when you go shopping.
- Keep your keys, wallet, and purse in a reusable tote bag at all times.

- Use a tote bag as your purse.
- As soon as you unpack your groceries, make sure to put the reusable bags back into their smart spots.
- Schedule a tote alarm on your phone. You don't have to tell people what it's for, and you might even seem cool and mysterious.
- Write "reusable bags" at the top of your shopping list so they're top of mind when you go to shop.
- Make your new "before I leave the house" chant: keys, wallet, phone, tote.
- Leave a reminder note somewhere very visible and close to the front door.

STARTER SUPPLIES

You really don't need much when it comes to supplies that'll help you waste less food and plastic. Buying more *anything* is not the goal here. By all means, skip over this section or rip it out and upcycle* the paper entirely if the idea of purchasing more things in order to waste less seems oxymoronic to you. That said, there are some items that can help reduce your reliance on single-use items and make your zero-waste aspirations go a little bit smoother.

---

* "Upcycle" means to transform materials that are no longer useful into something that gives them purpose. So, if you find the next few pages positively useless, here's permission to turn them into something of value, whether that's homemade wrapping paper, kindling for a fire, or pages for experimental doodling.

For Eating

- A reusable cutlery set that includes a fork, knife, spoon, chopsticks, and straw that you can use on the go to avoid plastic utensils (when you are inevitably given a plastic utensil set, feel free to return it to the restaurant or server).
- A reusable cup, mug, or tumbler that can store both hot and cold liquids for all of your hydration and caffeine needs.
- A couple of cloth napkins (two, so that you'll have one to use when you're washing the other). Feel free to repurpose cloth you've already got.
- Reusable snack bags for storage—Stasher Bags are one great option; there are plenty of other brands on the market.
- A few metal or glass containers for storing leftovers and packing lunch.

For Cleaning

In her book *Salt, Lemons, Vinegar, and Baking Soda*, Shea Zukowski details how to replace just about every household cleaning solution with a limited number of ingredients (bet you can guess which!).[6] The internet is also a great place to find recipes for natural cleaning solutions. If you want something pre-made, you can explore refill marketplaces (stores that allow you to bring your own containers to refill) or subscription services for soap and cleaning tablets that dissolve in water (Cleancult is one such brand); these are smart because they allow you to replenish your supplies without having to buy another plastic bottle.

Produce Cleanser

Since you'll be buying more loose produce and skipping plastic bags where you can, you'll want to be sure to wash your fruits and veggies. But you don't need to buy a solution from the store (that comes in a plastic bottle) to do so. Bonneau makes her own produce wash at home with baking soda and water. She advises mixing about a tablespoon of baking soda with six cups of water in a large bowl, then adding your produce to the bowl. Allow the produce to sit in the solution for about fifteen minutes, then drain the bowl and rinse and dry your food.

A 2017 study from the University of Massachusetts Amherst found that baking soda and water rid certain pesticides from fruit more effectively than a solution of bleach and water (what conventional produce wash tends to be made of).[7] Wash on.

Kitchen Sponges

Standard, disposable kitchen sponges are often made from oil-derived plastic. Worse, many contain microplastics—minuscule pieces of plastic—that go down the drain and end up in our water systems, where they're either eaten by marine animals or disrupt ocean life in other ways. At the end of a sponge's life—whenever its putrid kitchen-sponge smell becomes too much to bear—the item gets tossed in the trash and finds its way to the landfill, where it can remain intact for more than five hundred years. There are plenty of plastic-free sponge alternatives on the market. Real luffa sponges are made from the luffa plant and have a coarse, scrubby-like texture that's perfect for washing dishes. You can find these online or at many natural-food retailers. You can also grow them in your garden!

Besides the luffa, you can find earth-friendly sponges made from more sustainable materials like hemp, bamboo, vegetable cellulose, and much more. You can also make reusable, washable sponges from old towels. Just cut the towel into square pieces, then stack them in a kitchen drawer. Use them to scrub your dishes and countertops, and then toss them in the wash when it's time.

For Keeping Things Fresh

I can't think of anything more heartbreakingly sad than greens wilted too soon. Manufacturers suggest that a refrigerator's crisper will maintain the integrity of produce, but reality is often much soggier. Produce can rot more quickly than nature intended if it's improperly stored, but there are plenty of tools on the market that promise to preserve your produce, including:

- Airtight storage containers with ventilation and bottom trays to keep moisture from spoiling the goods (I have a few of these from Rubbermaid; they do seem to work, though they are bulky in the fridge).
- Cloth cotton bags meant to be kept damp while storing produce.
- Storage containers made specifically for various fruits and veggies (that usually come in the shape of said fruit or veggie).
- Silicone lids and covers to use instead of plastic wrap for storing cut produce.

WORKING WITH WHAT YOU'VE GOT

Just a little FYI—you don't have to toss all of your plastic stuff to achieve a #ZeroWaste aesthetic. Gorgeous, minimalist photos on Instagram may have you believing otherwise, but using what you already have is way better than forgoing it all for something new. "I think there's a huge disconnect in how we're defining zero waste," says Shilpi Chhotray. "It makes me uncomfortable that it's becoming this trendy, corporate commoditized business model." You can see evidence of zero waste as a lifestyle trend everywhere you look, with sleek, monochromatic bottles and jars signaling some kind of virtuous, aspirational living. Don't fall for it.

There are countless products that promise a cleaner, greener home. Before you add all of them to your cart, reassess the findings from your waste audit and figure out what items you're using the most. Maybe you're good at eating all of your groceries before they spoil, but you have a bad plastic wrap habit. In this case, you probably don't need special contraptions to keep your food fresh, but you might benefit from investing in reusable covers or storage bags.

3.

GREENWASHING AND THE MYTH OF CONSUMER CHOICE

*G*reenwashing, when a product is portrayed as good or better for the environment when there's really much more to the story, is nearly impossible to avoid in the modern grocery store. When a granola bar claims to be "healthy" or a bag of potato chips deems itself "all natural," what do these terms actually mean?

More often than not, they mean nothing.

Brands engage in greenwashing because doing so helps sell their products. This is a real bummer. On the bright side, greenwashing is a sign of changing consumer demand. "Greenwashing is often a direct result from the pressure people and policy makers are putting on corporations in demanding a food system that works for people and keeps people healthy," says Taylor Billings, press secretary for Corporate Accountability, an organization that challenges and changes destructive behaviors of corporations. The fact that brands are putting in effort to make us believe they're "green"—even if all they're doing is trying to fake us out—does show that our desires are being heard. This is progress, no matter how infinitesimal.

Billings said we wouldn't be seeing packaging that appears more eco-friendly or words like "natural" on food products if consumers weren't demanding a better food system. The problem is that we consumers are often duped by the greenwashing treatment. "The biggest problem with greenwashing is that, so often, [the claim] is just not true," Billings says. She adds that greenwashing slows down our progress, because the changes companies surrender to can be so pathetically incremental, it can be like pulling teeth. The greenwashing "tends to drag out how long these products are acceptable without companies needing to change their core business model or practices," says Billings.

The longer food companies make us believe that a green font indicates sustainability, the less real work they have to do to own up to their unsustainable practices.

Companies implement all kinds of strategies to convince consumers that their products are greener than they are. From beautiful imagery of nature to brand-dictated certifications to clickbait-like claims that lack scientific backing, marketers have mastered this kind of con-artistry.

Let's look at a real-life example. This one's a little complicated, but stay with me. Many of Nestlé USA's chocolate products include phrases like "sustainably sourced" and "supporting farmers for better chocolate," which lead at least some consumers to believe that the food is both sourced and produced responsibly.

But according to an April 2019 class-action lawsuit filed against the company, the cocoa is sourced from farms that implement child and slave labor and engage in a supply chain that has "virtually no environmental standards in place."[1] The complaint also charges the company with destroying rainforests in West Africa and using chemicals that pollute waterways, kill wildlife, and harm communities.

In 2001, Nestlé signed a protocol that signified it would commit to growing and processing cocoa beans without "the worst forms of child labor." More than a decade later, independent research from Tulane University found that child labor on the company's cocoa plantations had significantly increased. The suit goes on to cite the company's illegal deforestation practices, claiming that Nestlé's "Cocoa Plan," an internal certification plan that claims to be dedicated to better farming practices, is a "sham." Nestlé responded to the suit by producing a "Tackling Child Labor 2019 Report" document under its "Cocoa Plan." The document is heavy on beautiful images of children and messaging that highlights literacy, work, and education programs it has implemented for people in West Africa, as well as a promise that "by 2025, we aim to source 100 percent of our cocoa for our confectionery products through the Nestlé Cocoa Plan."[2] The Nestlé Cocoa Plan defines sustainability by its own criteria without objective third-party evaluations, which is, at the very least, pretty sneaky.

The Rainforest Alliance, a nonprofit corporation that stamps products with a little green frog, is another defendant in a greewashing-related lawsuit. The Rainforest Alliance certification process ostensibly identifies sustainable practices that support rainforests. In 2014, the Seattle-based Water and Sanitation Health group sued the Alliance for certifying Chiquita banana farms and allowing all Chiquita bananas to carry the Alliance's seal of approval.

WASH director Eric Harrison visited Rainforest Alliance–certified farms in Guatemala and witnessed "aerial fumigation over schools and homes" and "open-source rivers with no protection from the chemical fumigation," he told nonprofit organization Truth in Advertising.[3] "They are actually certifying farms that are not acting in an environmentally sustainable manner," Harrison said. "Anytime you see aerial fumigation over a school or home, you're kind of shocked that a certification body like Rainforest Alliance has put their seal of approval on it."

This instance of potential greenwashing is particularly egregious because it was implemented by a group that's meant to act as a safeguard. It'd be one thing if Chiquita had certified itself as rainforest-friendly (which would be similar to Nestlé's case), but this case of greenwashing is layered. Harrison put it best when he described the overall offense associated with greenwashing: "Consumers are trying to vote with their dollars by purchasing goods that are supposedly better for the environment," Harrison told the nonprofit, pro-consumer group Truth in Advertising. "We have companies taking advantage of that by using marketing claims that convince the consumer that they should purchase their product because of their environmental record." For the record, the Rainforest Alliance denied the allegations.[4] Groups in addition to WASH have criticized the Alliance for similar offenses.

These kinds of misleading marketing strategies are used frequently and can be tough to see through. It's beyond frustrating; how the hell are we supposed to know what's true when the bullshit is so strategically well placed? It's not easy, but to start, we have to question everything and be cautious of pretty much any claim that something is good for the planet. There's nothing inherently wrong with wanting to try an ingredient that marketers say will help you save the earth, lose weight, find happiness, and become wealthy. The problem comes when your expectations drive your purchases, fueling the monster that can keep up its tricks with your money in its pockets.

Fortunately, consumer-advocate groups are fighting for transparency and truth, questioning labels with little merit that still persuade consumers to make purchases. Watchdog groups like the Center for Science in the Public Interest, Truth in Advertising, Corporate Accountability, and many more are dedicated to pointing out corporate inconsistencies and making sure companies are kept liable. On an individual level, you'll be better prepared if you know how to see past the bullshit. You'll find some tips to do just that in the next chapter.

Producing junk science—often in the form of studies funded by industry groups to "prove" their products are healthy and better— is another tactic Big Food implements to draw in customers. These studies often get blasted by the media because they're salacious, prescriptive, or make for good headlines ("Eating Chocolate Is Good for Your Heart!"), but they rarely tell the whole truth, including the conflicts of interest that sparked the research in the first place ("This study is sponsored by Mars, maker of M&M's!"). Consumer beliefs can be heavily influenced by this type of storytelling (because who doesn't want to believe that chocolate is a health cure?).

THE MYTH OF CONSUMER CHOICE

The myth of consumer choice is another aspect of consumerism's current landscape that makes it pretty difficult to know what we're getting. Americans, in particular, pride themselves on the concept of choice—freedom!—and corporations thrive off marketing the perception of said choice. Emphasizing the importance of choice has actually helped companies sidestep responsibility. Corporations put their hands up in innocence, as if to say, "We just make [X heinous product], we don't force anyone to buy it!" In reality, some of the most successful brands shrewdly implement strategies to mess with consumers' psychology and lead them to buy what they're selling. Some would call this corporate abuse. As Alexa Kaczmarski of Corporate Accountability explained to me, our food system is built on this false perception that it's anyone's choice to buy a Snickers instead of a bag of carrots.

"There's so much baked into that and the privilege to actually make that choice," says Kaczmarski, noting how, first, multimillion-dollar campaigns are executed to make Snickers a desirable purchase and, also, how the less healthy "choice" is often the least expensive option. Sure, it's an American's "choice" to go to McDonald's instead of preparing an organic, veggie-centric meal at home, but how much of that "choice" is dictated by money, class, and resources?

"If a corporation is able to put the burden on the person, the corporation is in a much better position to not be held accountable for that," Kaczmarski explains.

At the grocery store, the average shopper has countless decisions to make. For example, you can choose a specific granola bar from dozens of brands; maybe you pay a little more to buy the one made with organic oats or splurge for one made without added sugars. Not everyone has such luxury, and for some, making healthier purchasing decisions isn't exactly a *choice*.

"Corporations have shaped a food system in which you have to be able to pay in order to not be poisoned," says Taylor Billings, also of Corporate Accountability. Indeed, we have to pay more to feel a little more secure that our foods weren't harvested by mistreated laborers, and we have to spend extra in hopes that our foods aren't contaminated with toxic chemicals.

The myth of consumer choice is heavy stuff, but at its core is this: most food products in the United States are marketed by just ten companies (including Coca-Cola, PepsiCo, and Nestlé).[5] It's these companies that choose how they market certain products, source ingredients, pay workers, and treat the environment. The more clearly we can recognize who's to blame, the more ammunition we have to demand change.

4.

LOOK OUT FOR THESE BULLSHIT LABELS

*W*hile advocacy groups work to fight behemoth brands and demand that they be more transparent, we all must be critical consumers. Food items that aggressively promote their benefits—whether for health, the planet, or anything in between—need to be met with doubt.

Don't just close your eyes and swallow. Instead, look out for labels and phrasing that hint at shadiness, and start following certifications that you trust (more on those in chapter 7). Below, find some words and phrases commonly found on food products and get familiar with their real meanings.

HEALTHY

Findings from a 2018 food and beverage survey found that 93 percent of consumers have the desire to eat healthy at least some of the time.[1] No surprise there. But what "healthy" means is truly up for interpretation, since the term suffers from some pretty vague food-industry guidelines. After years of drama, the Food and Drug Administration has started the process of redefining the word.[2] "Healthy" previously focused on a food's fat content, which meant that a snack cup of chocolate pudding could be labeled as healthy, while nutritional powerhouses like salmon and avocado missed the mark. That's beyond nonsense. While the FDA works to figure itself out, it will once again be up to the consumer to read between the lines. This is just one of many instances in which a label might actually do more harm than good.

Takeaway: Don't wait for the FDA to decide what "healthy" means. Do some reading and come up with your own definition, and ignore the "healthy" labels that are vying for your money.

NATURAL

Don't fall for this meaningless label. The term "natural" isn't regulated by the FDA (or any official group, for that matter), meaning that food companies can slap it on everything from candy corn to a bag of chips. Data from Nielsen finds that the food industry sells more than $40 billion worth of food labeled with the word "natural" every year.[3] Labels with "natural" or "all natural" often persuade consumers to spend. A 2019 survey conducted by Wakefield Research found that 53 percent of Americans would be motivated to purchase a product with a "natural" claim.[4] Wah.

Takeaway: Use common sense. Something that comes in a package is probably less "natural" than an apple, but even that is up for debate. Maybe just remove the word from your grocery-store lexicon.

SUPERFOOD/SUPERFRUIT

If you're buying something because it claims to contain "super-foods," you may be succumbing to some cheap marketing. While many foods are nutrient-packed and have great health benefits, the definition of "superfood" has been whittled down to a means of sell-ing. And consumers know it! Research in 2016 from the University of Adelaide's Food Values Research Group found that consumers are skeptical of this kind of marketing, and they are aware of false prom-ises, but they eat foods that are labeled to support their aspirations.[5] "Consumers are happy to succumb to a bit of magical thinking and eat superfoods as a sort of extra insurance, because they believe that these foods might help their health, and probably can't hurt," said Jessica Loye, the study's author.

Takeaway: Consider all vegetables and fruits super, and when you buy them sans packaging, consider yourself even more super.

PLANT-BASED

It's terrific that consumers are becoming more interested in plant-based foods, aka foods that are made out of plants rather than animals. Eating more plants and less meat can benefit both the planet's and humans' health. Still, be wary when products all but shout that they are plant-based. Plant-based does not mean healthy or better. Nachos can be plant-based. The plant-based "meats" that are popping up in just about every fast-food chain can have just as many grams of fat, sodium, and cholesterol as their animal-based counterparts. And while we know that, in general, the production of plants does less harm to the environment than the production of meat, there's not enough research to justify all of these new, trendy alternatives as better.

Takeaway: Eat plant-based foods that are naturally made from plants, without artificial additives.

SUSTAINABLE

Considering the title of this book, this one's ironic, I know. At this point, "sustainable" is more of a *vibe* than an identifier with actual criteria. Ask yourself what "sustainable" means in the context of the product, or *how* it's promoting sustainability before you buy into the claim.

Takeaway: Research brands' sustainability practices before you go shopping, and keep a list of the brands that support what you believe in.

BIOPLASTIC OR BIO-BASED PLASTIC

First, a little background. Plastics are made up of molecules called polymers. Polymers contain carbon, which gives plastic some of its properties. Most things on earth are made of carbon—including humans—so this is not particularly unique. "Bio-based" refers to where carbon is sourced from, says Ramani Narayan, University Distinguished Professor, Michigan State University. When "bio" is in the name, the carbon comes from renewable plant resources, rather than petroleum resources (fossil fuels). You'd think that plastic sourced from plants would always be preferable to plastic sourced from greenhouse-gas-producing fuels, but it's not that simple, says Narayan.

Bioplastic doesn't necessarily decompose back into the earth effortlessly. So don't let the marketing trick steer your green intentions down the wrong path. Context is crucial here. As Narayan puts it, carbon sourced from plant resources does offer value, but what's key is what happens to the bio-based plastic item at the *end* of its life. If it can be composted or recycled, that's a great quality (see just below for BPI labeling). But if it cannot, and a similar product made from petroleum-based plastic can, it's not clear as to which is "better." Variables associated with the product matter as much as the material itself. This is all to say that you shouldn't choose a product exclusively because it touts its bio-based materials. It can often be a better alternative, but this isn't always true.

Takeaway: Try to stick to packaging that can be recycled or, better yet, composted.

BIODEGRADABLE

"Biodegradable is one of the most misused and abused terms," says Narayan. As with "bio-based," the word "biodegradable" is pretty meaningless without context. "Everything is biodegradable," Narayan points out, because everything breaks down. The important qualifiers are the extent and rate of the degradation, he says. The Federal Trade Commission issues "Green Guides" that advise marketers on the meanings of certain environmental claims.[6] In order for marketers to claim biodegradability "without saying more," as the FTC puts it, there must be proof that "the product will break down and return to nature within a year."

Over the years, the FTC has "warned" manufacturers that their environmental claims may be deceptive to consumers. "If marketers don't have reliable scientific evidence for their claims, they shouldn't make them," Jessica Rich, director of the FTC's Bureau of Consumer Protection, said in a 2014 press release.[7] "Claims that products are environmentally friendly influence buyers, so it's important they be accurate."

To be really sure that packaging is biodegradable, Narayan suggests turning to the Biodegradable Products Institute, North America's leading certifier of compostable products and packaging. When you see a "BPI-Compostable" label on packaging, you can be pretty confident the product is safe for composting and will naturally break down in the environment within a year's time. BPI's website also provides a service where you can check to see if your favorite products are certified.

Takeaway: Look for the BPI-Compostable label.

DEGRADABLE

The word "degradable" implies that something will break down. That's it. Garbage bags and plastic water bottles may be marketed as degradable, and that means they will break down into smaller pieces over time. Degradation is a process that fuels the increase in microplastics; when something like a plastic bag degrades, it breaks down into smaller pieces. But just because you can't necessarily *see* those smaller pieces doesn't mean they don't exist. To put it poetically, degradable is just a really dumb term.

Takeaway: Just ignore this terminology.

5.

HOW TO CUT BACK
ON FOOD WASTE

We waste a grotesque amount of food. One-third of the world's food supply gets tossed, which is enough food to feed two billion people. According to the United Nations, it equates to an economic loss of around $750 billion.[1] Americans spend around $218 billion on the 40 percent of food that never gets eaten in America. A staggering 58 percent of all the food produced in Canada is wasted or lost; calculations estimate that, with the right systems and desire, a third could be rescued and given to Canadians in need.[2] These numbers are hard to swallow. Our food habits and purchasing decisions are intricately tied to the health of the planet and the people living on it.

Food waste is problematic not just because excess food can help the hungry, but because of what happens to the waste when it decomposes. A big misconception about food scraps is that they break down naturally as garbage. In reality, about 95 percent of the food we discard goes to landfills or combustion facilities, where it does break down, but instead of providing full-circle nutrients back to the earth, it produces methane, a greenhouse gas that contributes to earth's rising temperatures. Whether an onion peel, a piece of rotten fruit, or the skin of a carrot, this is the fate of the food we trash. By some estimates, food waste around the world accounts for 10 percent of all greenhouse gas emissions.[3]

A SILVER LINING

Half of the food waste that happens in the world happens in our very own homes. So, while it often feels like there's nothing we can personally do to tackle climate change, which needs to be addressed systemically, reducing how much food we waste is something we *can* start tackling on our own. And it *will* matter. Reducing food waste is the third most viable solution for reducing greenhouse gases (and thus climate change), according to Project Drawdown, a research organization that works to identify global climate solutions.[4]

There are many simple things we can all do to waste less food. In the United States, the most commonly wasted foods include bread, vegetables (bagged salad is a big culprit!), fruit, meat, poultry, dairy, and fish.[5]

This is not a food-waste recipe book (these do exist, if you're intrigued), but here are a few things you could do with foods that usually go to waste.

BREAD

- Freeze half your loaf. Frozen bread turns into fantastic toast.
- Make your own bread crumbs or croutons from days-old or stale bread.
- Look up "bread pudding recipes." Whether you prefer sweet or savory, I promise you'll find something that appeals to you.
- Eat more sandwiches.

PRODUCE

- If you find lots of unused produce in your waste audit, consider trading at least a few of your wasted buys for frozen versions. Frozen fruit and vegetables are often less expensive than fresh, and, of course, they last longer. It's mostly untrue that frozen produce has fewer nutritional benefits, so don't hold back.
- Make a jam or compote with really ripe fruit.
- Give fresh herbs like dill, oregano, basil, and mint a whole new life by freezing the extras in oil in an ice-cube tray (to do this, blend about a cup of herbs with ¼ cup of oil or butter in your food processor). You will never be mad to remember you have a fancy oil to cook with for stir-fries, soups, and dips. Don't forget to label these.

- Peel and freeze super-soft bananas for a wonderfully sweet future banana bread.
- Celery gets its own bullet point because soup often calls for a few stalks of celery, and yet I find it impossible to purchase fewer than six stalks. Some ways to prevent the remaining stalks from getting old and bendy:
  - Chop up the leftover produce and freeze it for a future soup (you can do the same with onions and other soup staples).
  - Make celery soup with milk and/or potatoes/onions that are also on their way out.
  - Stick a stalk in a homemade cocktail (Bloody Marys aren't the only option, but they are a great one).
  - Use the leaves in a salad; they're both edible and tasty!
- Quit buying bagged lettuce and salad mixes (more on that in chapter 6).

EXTENDING THE LIFE OF YOUR PRODUCE

More important than fancy kitchen gadgets is the knowledge of how to store your food in the first place. Some basic guidelines:

- Potatoes, tomatoes, shallots, and onions are not fridge foods! Keep them out of the refrigerator, but do store them in a cool, dry place. They'll spoil more quickly in plastic bags. Once cut, store them in a resealable bag or container in the refrigerator.
- Unripe fruit will ripen more quickly on the counter. Transfer it to the refrigerator once it's soft.
- Citrus fruits can be stored on the counter, but they'll last longer in the fridge.
- If your produce bounty has a moldy or rotten outlier, remove it from the bunch and compost it. The rest of the food has a better shot at keeping fresh with it gone.

Not all fruits and veggies do well when stored together. Certain types release ethylene gas, which causes produce to ripen faster. A basic rule of thumb here: ethylene-sensitive fruits and vegetables should not be stored near fruits and vegetables that produce ethylene.[6] So everything in the first column of the chart on page 36 should be kept away from anything listed in the second column. Doing so will extend the life of your produce, though stashing an apple and a banana in the same bowl isn't going to cause any drastic drama; you'll just want to plan to eat them sooner.

You want to give your produce some breathing room, especially when you intend for it to last. This means that you should avoid storing ethylene-producing fruits and veggies in sealed containers or the plastic bags you may have taken them home in; the bags trap ethylene gas and accelerate ripening.

You can also use the power of ethylene to ripen foods faster. To hasten the softening of a rock-hard avocado, place it in a brown paper bag alongside an apple. Since apples are ethylene producers, the gas will affect the avocado and speed up its ripening process.

Ethylene Producers

- Apples
- Avocados
- Bananas
- Cantaloupes
- Kiwis
- Peaches
- Pears
- Peppers
- Tomatoes

Ethylene Sensitive

- Apples
- Asparagus
- Avocados
- Bananas
- Broccoli
- Cantaloupes
- Collard Greens
- Cucumbers
- Eggplants

Ethylene-Sensitive Produce (Continued)

- Grapes
- Honeydew
- Honey Don't
- Kiwis
- Lemons
- Limes
- Mangoes
- Onions
- Peaches
- Peppers
- Pears
- Squash
- Sweet Potatoes
- Watermelons

Composting

Composting can be a great alternative to throwing away food. When food gets tossed in the trash, it eventually makes its way to landfills, where it takes up space and, without much oxygen access, releases methane into the atmosphere. When food is composted correctly, the compost can be added to soil to help plants grow, and the amount of methane released is drastically reduced.

Indoor composting bins won't smell or attract bugs as long as they're properly maintained. There are two main types of indoor composting. *Aerobic composting* uses garden soil to convert scraps into compost, which can then be used as plant fertilizer. *Vermicomposting* is similar, but the addition of worms (contained, don't worry!) helps speed up the process and adds even more nutrients to the soil.[7] There are resources online for composting care and maintenance; soon enough, you'll be a pro.

For composting outdoors, you'll want to keep a compost bin

or pile in a dry, shady spot near a water source (like a hose). The EPA recommends chopping or shredding larger pieces (they'll break down more quickly this way), and moistening dry materials every time you add them. You'll also want to bury fruit and vegetable waste underneath yard waste.

Some cities have composting programs, often at farmers' markets or other community-sponsored events, and some have curbside composting services that will pick up your scraps and take them to industrial composting facilities. In between pickup times, you can store your food scraps in the freezer, where they won't stink up your kitchen. Once you start composting, you might be surprised to see how much waste you collect.

MATERIALS THAT CAN GO INTO YOUR COMPOST
All of this information comes from the EPA.[8]

- Fruits and vegetables
- Eggshells
- Nut shells
- Tea bags
- Coffee grounds and filters
- Bread products
- Shredded newspaper
- Cardboard
- Paper
- Houseplants
- Leaves
- Yard trimmings
- Grass clippings
- Hay and straw
- Dryer and vacuum-cleaner lint
- Fireplace ashes
- Sawdust
- Wood chips
- Hair and fur
- Cotton and wool rags

MATERIALS YOU CANNOT COMPOST

Composting rules vary, so be sure to check with your local program.

- Black walnut tree leaves or twigs
- Coal or charcoal ash
- Dairy products
- Diseased or insect-ridden plants
- Fats, grease, lard, or oils
- Meat or fish bones and scraps
- Pet poop and cat litter wastes (e.g., dog or cat feces, soiled cat litter)
- Yard trimmings treated with chemical pesticides

If you get big into this composting thing, maybe you can get other people on board. You might consider taking the process to work or school to grow your impact exponentially. If you think *you* produce a lot of organic waste, think about the amount that must be created in office lunchrooms and school cafeterias.

ANIMALS

Not all food waste is created equal. By volume, more fruits and veg-etables are wasted than meat products. Still, research suggests that meat waste has a much more significant environmental impact than does produce. "Beef represents the largest contribution to post-consumer [greenhouse gas] emissions embodied in food waste," write the authors of a University of Missouri College of Agriculture, Food and Natural Resources study published in the journal *Renew-able Agriculture and Food Systems.*[9]

To waste less meat:

- Buy less meat to begin with. You can supplement a meal with grains, starches, and vegetables.
- Freeze meat. Just make sure to fully seal the meat, so moisture can't get in. The US Depart-ment of Agriculture recommends keeping un-cooked roasts, steaks, and chops up to a year in the freezer, and uncooked ground meat for up to four months.
- Refreeze meat. The USDA says it's safe to refreeze thawed meat.[10]
- Don't fear freezer burn. Freezer burn does not mean the meat can't be consumed. It's just a sign that some sections may be a little dry.
- Don't let a power outage ruin your life. According to the USDA, "a freezer full of food will usually keep about two days if the door is kept shut; a half-full freezer will last about a day." If the freezer

isn't full, you can group the frozen packages together so they better retain their cold. The USDA recommends separating meat and poultry from other frozen foods, so if they do begin to thaw, they won't contaminate your ice cream.

- Take stock of the meat in your freezer *before* you head to the butcher or grocery store. Plan a day or two ahead, and transfer meat from freezer to fridge so it can safely thaw.

DAIRY

- Learn how to read expiration dates (see page 42).
- Move dairy products with shorter shelf lives to the front of the refrigerator.
- Consider reducing your milk, cheese, and other dairy-based food consumption; the market is rife with alternatives that are gentler on the planet (see chapter 9 on buying milk).

THE NOTORIOUSLY CONFUSING SELL-BY DATES

Dates that mark food products are often more suggestion than law, but both consumer and retail confusion about what these dates mean has led to a lot of food waste. The USDA's Food Safety and Inspection Service writes that foods (excluding infant formula) are safe to eat after the date passes. "Spoiled foods will develop an off odor, flavor, or texture due to naturally occurring spoilage bacteria," according to the USDA.[11] "If a food has developed such spoilage characteristics, it should not be eaten."

In other words, there's really nothing wrong with the smell test. You'll know.

There are small differences in the meanings of "use by," "sell by," "best by," and "best if used by/before," but the best test is your nose.

SOME OTHER PRACTICAL PLACES TO ADJUST

Since the majority of us are guilty of waste, we could start by just buying less at the grocery store. If you're a meal planner, plan for a few meals that revolve around leftovers. Even if you're not much of a planner, make leftover nights or "kitchen sink nights" part of your eating repertoire. Take stock of your pantry and fridge before you pick a recipe or head to the grocery store, and don't be afraid to substitute ingredients for what you have on hand (rice bowls, for example, can be made with quinoa instead, truly!).

In her book *Scraps, Peels, and Stems: Recipes and Tips for Rethinking Food Waste at Home*, author Jill Lightner makes the case for buying greens with "sturdier leaves," particularly if wilted lettuce is a big factor in your waste audit.[12] "There's a fairly obvious rule to keep in mind, which is that the sturdier the leaf, the longer it will last in the fridge," writes Lightner. "All varieties of kale and cabbage will last the longest; chard and bok choy are in the middle; lettuces of all sorts, whether they're whole heads or bagged as a mix, and tender herbs (the kind that we eat the stems of) are the most perishable." If you're always tossing out delicate baby lettuces, maybe it's time to switch to greens that are more likely to hold up to your forgetting you bought them in the first place.

REFRAMING YOUR PERSPECTIVE ON "WASTE"

In my household, I find myself too often clearing the fridge of weeks-old rice, wilted herbs, sad, soft celery stalks, and other neglected consumables. I think part of wasting less involves reframing our perspective on waste. Before it goes bad, can you reframe the food you'd normally toss as **"opportunity"**? There's great potential in the foods we waste—often left over from excess recipe ingredients or meals made too big—to be turned into meals of their own. With just a little out-of-the-box creative thinking, some wimpy remains from the week can be transformed into a satiating grain bowl, veggie stir-fry, or inventive salad. Not everything you cook needs to stem from a recipe or constitute that misleading concept of a "meal." If it fills you up, tastes good, and helps you reduce your waste, consider it a success.

6.

HOW TO NAVIGATE
THE PRODUCE AISLE

There's no hard-and-fast rule for what makes one apple "better" than another. I wish grocery shopping could be that prescriptive, but there are an infinite number of factors that come into play, ones that soar far beyond whether something is organic.

Sustainable food isn't just food that's good for the environment. Sustainable food has to be good for the people responsible for getting it from the ground to the shelves and, if you don't want to fall for greenwashing claims, this is really critical to keep in mind.

As part of its marketing smarts, one of Big Food's most used tactics is to "create distance between where your food comes from and how it ends up on the grocery store shelf," says Taylor Billings, of Corporate Accountability. When you don't see how your food gets made and who suffers during the process, you're more likely to experience cognitive dissonance, and to make the purchase.

There are mixed opinions about whether organic is "best," but one concept experts seem to agree on is that buying local—whether through farmers' markets or CSA (Community Supported Agriculture) programs—is a reliable way to know that at least *some* sustainable practices have been employed to produce your food. So, oddly enough, you might want to take your produce shopping outside of the grocery store.

"It's really good to get close to the people who grow your food," says Lena Brook, director of food campaigns for the Natural Resources Defense Council. Purchasing food from these types of local vendors circumvents the need to spend money with mass producers who tend to care more about profit than process.

GOING LOCAL

Eating local foods may not reduce your carbon footprint as much as once believed (new research highlights that the *type* of food you eat has a much more significant impact on the environment than how far a food had to travel to get to you).[1] Still, there are plenty of benefits to eating food that was produced close to home. Buying local foods in season supports the local economy; research shows that money spent on local farmers stays in the community and is reinvested in the local economy. One 2016 report from the University of California, Davis, found that "for every dollar of sales . . . direct marketers are generating twice as much economic activity within the region, as compared to producers who are not involved in direct marketing."[2] Furthermore, the study found that for every $1 million in revenue, local farms and growing markets create almost 32 local jobs, whereas larger wholesale growers create 10.5.

"When I think about my food dollars, the best way for me to get them into the hands of people who do the right thing is to give them to farmers," says Urvashi Rangan, chief scientist at Grace Communications, an organization working to build public awareness of the critical environmental and public health issues created by the current industrial food system.

An extra perk of going local is that you meet face-to-face. Local growers can tell you how the food was grown. Consumers can ask questions, like what practices farmers use to harvest their crops, and be more confident in the answer since it's coming straight from the source (unlike at the supermarket).

There's even some research that suggests that locally grown food is healthier because it retains more nutrients.[3] Plus, foods from local growers are more likely to contain fewer pesticides compared with those from industrialized farms, or none at all, even if they're not certified organic.

Of course, not everyone has access to these local programs (though it's worth doing some research—try localharvest.org), and sometimes it can seem that produce at farmers' markets is more expensive than store-bought food (research shows, however, that this is rarely the case).

GOING ORGANIC

The word "organic" elicits all kinds of feelings. Some people can't shake organic foods' elitist reputation, unable to separate its potential benefits from higher price tags and, yeah, elitist marketing. Others equate organic with "better," without a real grasp of what better means in the context of food. Whatever your take, it's worth knowing how organic food actually differs from its conventionally grown counterpart.

Organic produce is grown without the use of synthetic fertilizers or pesticides—this fact alone is sometimes enough for people to choose organic. Synthetic fertilizers and pesticides are commonly sourced from fossil fuels, which emit greenhouse gases that are partly responsible for climate change. Organic farming does rely on pesticides and the like, but these are sourced from naturally occurring materials. Does natural mean better? Not necessarily. Research on organic pesticides is in constant motion, and certain types have been found to be dangerous and continue to be banned, or at least reconsidered.[4]

Organic tends to be more costly than food produced through conventional farming, and even proponents of organic don't deny this; instead, they place blame on the chaotic inner workings of the imperfect food system. "The way our food system works is that there are tons of subsidies in play, and most of those subsidies are going to grain and corn and soy producers," says Lena Brook. "The economic dynamics of the food systems are really complicated, and our food is artificially cheap." (This last bit gets at the idea that it's generally messed up that a bag of potato chips tends to be cheaper than an actual potato.) "The reality of what people face at checkout is real," Brook continues. She recommends, especially for low-income buyers, shopping for in-season food available at farmers' markets, if they are accessible.

And still, organic doesn't always mean better for the environment, either. In some instances, organic farms may require more land than conventional ones—an environmental drawback.[5] An organic label on its own can't indicate whether a food has a decreased environmental impact.

As much as we'd like for it to be the case, simple binaries like "good" and "bad" don't really exist when it comes to food. "Organic farming has many advantages, but it doesn't solve all the environmental problems associated with producing food," said Stefan Wirsenius, an associate professor at Chalmers University of Technology, who contributed to a 2018 study that found organic peas farmed in Sweden had 50 percent higher emissions compared with peas that were conventionally grown in the country.[6]

At some point during organic's boom, the belief that organic food is healthier—as in, more nutritious—began to form. This just has not been proven.[7]

We could easily go around and around about whether organic is better, because "better" is such a subjective term and there is a host of conflicting research about organic farming's impact. A recent position staked out in this debate underscores the benefit of "regenerative organic agriculture," farming practices that not only focus on the source of pesticides but also prioritize the health of farm soil, workers, and animals.[8] The concept is really well depicted in the 2019 documentary The Biggest Little Farm, in which virtually everything grown or living on the farm serves some kind of symbiotic process that provides a kind of circular sustenance.[9] It's a beautiful process that also seems utopic when compared with industrialized farming practices. Advocates expect Regenerative Organic Certification to become increasingly popular in food, but, depending on your stance, it could just come across as another confusing food label.

There is much more to say about organic versus conventional and all of the many nuances in between, but I think the most important takeaway from the debate is this: our food system is flawed. The answer to whether organic is better is unsatisfying and complex: it just depends.

Well, that was not fun and not really helpful, huh? I feel you. Whether you buy organic or not, there are some other, more actionable tips to keep in mind when produce shopping. Let's get into it.

THREE THINGS TO AVOID IN THE PRODUCE AISLE

1. Pre-packaged fruit and veggies. They are generally more expensive than naked produce, and the plastic wrap and Styrofoam are needless extras, especially when nature created a (compostable!) package all on its own. Still, there's no need to shame here—there will always be a person who could really benefit from a peeled orange wrapped in plastic, but that person is probably not you.

    Worse than the surcharge, pre-cut produce is actually a synonym for bacteria utopia.[10] This "convenience food" has been linked to salmonella outbreaks and other kinds of health risks because once the skin is broken, the flesh is that much more prone to being contaminated.

2. Using plastic produce bags for every loose kiwi. If you're grossed out by the idea of your food touching the store's conveyor belt, just know that it's been transported on the equivalent of a New York City subway floor in order to get to the grocery store in the first place. You might instead bring a few extra cloth bags to keep smaller pieces of pro-

duce from rolling away or getting crushed. If you do end up using those plastic baggies provided by grocers, do your best to reuse them at the store in the future. They can usually withstand a few rounds, so long as you're gentle with them.

3. Being vain. The reason there's usually a bounty of delightful freshness awaiting your relishing glance at the grocery store is because consumers love to see it. Grocers have found that overflowing displays of bright, edible merchandise are most appealing to us, which inevitably leads to waste. Turns out no one wants to buy the last apple on display. Consumers are also enticed by blemish-free produce, so a well-curated produce section is considered one in which the fruit and veg are symmetrical to one another and fairly uniform in color. We basically apply conventional, unrealistic beauty standards to our food, which is, at the very least, inane. One study reports that approximately half of all produce in the United States goes to waste because it's not considered beautiful.[11]

There has been a surge in rescue efforts to protect the ugly ducklings of the produce aisle; groups like the "Ugly" Fruit and Veg campaign have convinced retailers to sell so-called ugly produce at discounted prices, while other companies have added do-good elements to their marketing portfolio by turning misshapen produce into juice and other products. The least we can do is enjoy the weird in the world and buy a pepper even if it's shaped like a human butt.

BIG BAD BAGGED LETTUCE

I'll admit, washing lettuce is very annoying. But pre-washed, bagged lettuce can be both vile and bad. Here's why:

- Because bagged greens are washed, you probably won't wash them again when you're ready to eat them. But the words "triple-washed" and "pre-washed" don't guarantee clean. One study conducted by the University of California, Riverside, found that more than 90 percent of bacteria on triple-washed baby spinach leaves actually thrived on the leaves because of the shape and crevices of the leaves.[12] Similarly, a 2010 *Consumer Reports* test found that "not enough is being done to assure the safety or cleanliness of leafy greens," according to Michael Hansen, a senior scientist at Consumers Union.[13] *Consumer Reports* tested greens that came packaged in both bags and clamshells—those plastic containers that fold closed—and found that, in 39 percent of the samples, the amount of bacteria exceeded the level deemed acceptable by the FDA. Whether the products came in a bag or a clamshell or were organic or conventional made no difference in the levels of the bacteria.

- The packaged stuff costs way more than loose leaves or a head of something. Most Americans aren't eating enough greens as it is, so I hate to dissuade you from doing something good for yourself. Pre-washed lettuce is convenient, but you better bet that convenience comes with a price tag. The Simple Dollar, a financial education website, estimates that shoppers cough up an extra $2.90 for their lettuce to be washed and shredded for them.[14]

- Bagged greens are often left to die. A study focused around British consumers found that 40 percent of purchased bagged salads get tossed every year.[15] Pre-packaged leaves are seemingly just as easy to buy as they are to throw away. While I haven't come across any conclusive evidence, anecdotally I've experienced packaged greens produce a rancid, undrinkable green juice at the bottom of the bag far more quickly than a free leaf appears to turn.

7.

HOW TO BUY MEAT

I'm not going to tell you to become a vegan. Evidence does suggest that cutting meat and dairy from your diet could have a powerful effect on the planet. But—but!—even if you hold your cheeseburger dear and know for certain that you're not giving it up, you can still make a difference by choosing better meat (and, yeah, generally eating less of it).

You probably already know that eating less meat is better for the environment and your own health, and you find yourself glazing over when presented with the statistics that prove it. Maybe your traditions, your culture, everything that's important to you, is centered around meat, rooted in sharing an animal-based meal with people you love. So, for you, curtailing the amount of meat and dairy you consume is something that's much easier said than done. Let's just take a moment to recognize that, and recognize that choosing to eat less of these foods may sometimes feel challenging. It's okay if this is true.

Now for a moment of possible Zen: maybe you don't have to see your commitment to eating less meat as deprivation—like something is being taken away from you. Eating less meat means you have to be eating *more* of something else—and that can be a lot of fun, very delicious, and an entirely new adventure.

Try to do away with the notion that meat is always the best option or most important pick on the menu. Melissa Clark, a *New York Times* food columnist and self-proclaimed meat lover, has adopted this attitude in order to cut back on meat in her own life.[1] "On the upside," she writes, "eating less meat and dairy means there is more room on my plate for other delectable things: really good sourdough bread slathered with tahini and homemade marmalade, mushroom bourguignon over a mound of noodles, and all those speckled heirloom beans I keep meaning to order online."

JUST A FEW NUMBERS FOR CONTEXT

So, here goes. Out of all the ways to reduce our individual carbon footprints, eating less meat is arguably the greatest contribution you can make on an individual scale.[2] Consuming a diet rich in plants can help reduce emissions, and is generally thought to be healthier, resulting in a lower risk for chronic diseases.

Food production accounts for one-quarter of global greenhouse gas emissions, and the meat and dairy industries are a big reason why.[3] The two sectors contribute 14.5 percent of emissions, equivalent to the emissions produced by all planes, trucks, cars, and ships combined.[4]

Of all protein-rich foods, beef has the heftiest carbon footprint, followed by lamb. The greenhouse gas emissions associated with getting beef from the farm to your plate are enormous. Most emissions are a result of the amount of land required to raise and care for the animals, the application of fertilizers (both organic and synthetic) on this land, and cattle's own biological production of methane. For the sake of comparison, here's a fact: producing one kilogram of beef emits sixty kilograms of greenhouse gases, while producing one kilogram of, say, peas emits just one kilogram of gases.[5]

Temperatures are rising faster than we'd once thought and, according to the United Nations' 2018 climate report, the world will be in "crisis" by 2040.[6] (This crisis includes weather extremes—extreme drought and extreme flooding.) The report says that choosing to eat less meat is one thing we can do to make a real difference, and it's especially empowering because we don't need to rely on industry or government participation to make it happen.

We can't talk about eating meat without talking about the abominable distress and affliction animals endure for us to consume them. Selfishly, this is not a topic I care to dwell on because it physically hurts my heart, but to skip over it would be negligent.

"Farmed animals raised throughout the meat, dairy, and egg industries are tragically exploited," writes the Animal Legal Defense Fund.[7] "While some malicious abuse violates the law, much of the cruelty consists of commonplace industry practices—such as physical mutilations without anesthesia and the use of body-gripping cages and crates—that, while imposing pain and suffering, are legally tolerated." Investing your dollars in meat that comes from animals treated more humanely (more on that below) can help to set better standards and communicates to producers what consumers want.

"QUALITY" MEATS EXPLAINED

Now, as for the meat you *do* purchase: greenwashing is just as fla-grant at the butcher counter as it is in the snack aisle, so don't let your defenses ease you into buying a pricey pound of beef just be-cause it's labeled as grass-fed. The meaning of "quality meat" is pretty subjective, but in general, consumers want their steaks and chickens to come from animals that weren't pumped with antibiotics, weren't subjected to abuse, and didn't spend their lives on crowded, earth-polluting factory farms.

Meat can come with so many labels that the information ceases to be helpful—grass-fed, organic, natural—the terminology is often meaningless. To add even more confusion to the mix, some labels imply benefits to the environment; some suggest benefits relating to the animal, and others indicate benefits to consumers. It's really up to you to decide which is most important.

While there's no perfect system that promises your meat lives up to your standards 100 percent of the time, here are certain steps you can take to ensure that your meat is closer to what you want:

- Look for third-party certification: when buying meat, look for labels that include backing from trustworthy programs (more on this later).[8]
- Research brands and pick a few favorites that meet your standards. This will make it easier to shop.
- Know your meat label terminology (see next page), but don't have blind faith in it.
- Cross-reference label claims with help from apps. The Environmental Working Group has a "label

decoder" that can help you decipher false claims. Food Labels Exposed, an app from A Greener World, can also help you suss out something meaningful despite the bullshit.

- Ask questions. Ask your butcher what you're really getting from a certain product. Even if they don't know the answer, your asking reinforces the notion that consumers are hungry for transparency.

The following are some of the most common meat labels and the meanings behind them.

Grass-Fed

Grass-fed means that the animal was fed grass (or hay) for the majority of its life. According to the USDA, to qualify as grass-fed, the animal must have "continuous access to pasture during the growing season." Grass-fed beef tends to be *a bit* more nutritious than conventional (it contains, on average, just a little more omega-3 fat content), but not by any extreme measure.[9]

Grass-fed does not mean organic. The USDA's label refers to the animal's diet alone and does not refer to whether it received hormones or antibiotics.

Is grass-fed better for the environment? This is really unclear—you'll get different answers depending on whom you ask. When you really slice and dice it, though, eating any type of beef isn't doing the planet any favors right now.

Natural

Womp, womp. You'd hope that the meat you're buying is "natural," aka "real." If only we didn't need to specify. Meat and poultry can be labeled as natural so long as they contain "no artificial ingredient or added color and is only minimally processed," according to the USDA.[10] "Minimally processed" means that "the product was processed in a manner that does not fundamentally alter the product." Vague, isn't it? Producers must share the meaning of the term "natural" (with lines like "no artificial ingredients" or "minimally processed"), and that's as far as regulating goes.

Organic

This label means that the animal was raised on a certified organic farm, where the land hasn't been treated with most synthetic fertilizers and pesticides, sewage sludge, or genetic engineering for at least three years.[11] Animals marked as organic must be given access to the outdoors, space for exercise, and fresh air. According to the USDA, "organic management reduces stress, reducing the incidence of diseases and supporting animal welfare."

Raised without Antibiotics

This one's straightforward: the animal was not given antibiotics, not in its food or water or through injections. There is strong evidence that the use of antibiotics in animals is linked to resistant infections in humans, according to the CDC.[12]

Raised without Hormones

These animals have not received additional hormones throughout their lives (all animals have naturally occurring hormones). Added hormones are used to make animals grow faster—a practice that's banned in Europe based on concerns that consuming animals with growth hormones can be a health risk. In the United States, research concludes that the amount of most of the growth hormones present in these animals is too low to have a significant impact, but there are ongoing studies.[13]

Humanely Raised

Sounds nice, but there is no legal definition for this term, nor is there any on-farm inspection to verify the correct use of the claim. So consider this meaningless. Look to some of the third-party certifications (page 62) to learn which labels imply better treatment of animals. This description is an obvious case of humane-washing, a tactic producers and retailers use to make consumers believe they're purchasing animals that were treated in less-abusive conditions. There are plenty of ways to execute humane-washing tactics, whether its terminology like "responsibly raised" or "family farm" or images that depict happy animals roaming freely on green pastures. Consumers, beware.

Pasture-Raised

Animals that are pasture-raised must be given access to the outdoors for at least 120 days out of the year. The USDA requires labels to qualify what the term means at every individual farm, since some might provide pasture in a spacious field, while others may provide much smaller spaces. It can sometimes be tough to really visualize what the qualifying terminology is referring to, so if you want to make sure the animal had a better quality of life, look to third-party labels (see below) that recognize animal welfare.

No Nitrates/Nitrites Added

The USDA requires documentation from producers in order to use this claim. Nitrates and nitrites are preservatives that prevent harmful bacteria from growing. They also enhance color and sometimes add a smoky flavor. Many processed meats, including lunch meats, bacon, and hot dogs, are treated with nitrates, which have been found to increase the risk of cancer and other health problems, according to the Environmental Working Group. The claim does not mean that the product is completely free of nitrates or nitrites. There are naturally occurring sources of nitrite, like celery powder, that are added to most of these products. The product should be labeled with the qualifying statement, "except for those naturally occurring in" and then state the natural source.

THIRD-PARTY CERTIFICATIONS

Finding third-party certifications on your meat labels can be a helpful way to confirm you know what you're getting.[14] These aren't ironclad, but they do add an extra layer of protection against false claims. The following information is outlined by the EWG.

American Grassfed Association

Applicable to: beef, bison, lamb, goat, sheep, milk

In order to earn this certification, animals must be raised primarily on pasture with daily access to fresh air. They can only be fed grass and forage and are prohibited from grain feeding and GMO-based feed. The animals can't be given antibiotics (sick animals have to be treated, but they no longer qualify for certification). This certification does not involve any audits to ensure humane slaughter, nor does it have standards to minimize painful physical treatment (like tail docking or castration).

Animal Welfare Approved

Applicable to: beef, bison, lamb, goat, milk, pork, turkey, chicken, eggs, duck, geese, mutton

This label certifies that the animals were raised with continuous access to outdoor pasture. The label prohibits giving healthy animals antibiotics, though sick animals must be treated and can then be certified. Painful physical alterations, including tail docking, beak trimming, and more, are prohibited, and slaughter facilities are audited. GMO-based feed is not recommended under this certification, but it is allowed.

Certified Humane

Applicable to: beef, bison, lamb, goat, milk, pork, turkey, chicken, eggs

Under this certification, beef (but not dairy) cows must have continuous access to outdoor pasture (there are no outdoor requirements for other animals). No animals can be confined in cages or crates, and there are specific minimum amounts of space per animal. No antibiotics can be given to healthy animals, though sick animals must be treated and then can be certified. Slaughter facilities are audited. GMO-based feed is allowed, as is some use of feedlots. There are various standards in place to minimize painful physical alterations, but beak trimming and teeth clipping are prohibited.

USDA Organic

Applicable to: beef, lamb, goat, milk,
pork, turkey, chicken, eggs

Under this certification, animals must have year-round access to the outdoors, fresh air, and direct sunlight. Cows, sheep, and goats specifically must have access to pasture. USDA Organic requires pasture management to maximize soil fertility, prohibits GMO-based feed, and requires animals to be fed only certified organic feed. Antibiotics are not allowed, and sick animals must be treated and are no longer eligible to be certified. The standard for painful physical alterations is pretty vague under this label, requiring that it be done "in a manner that minimizes pain and stress." There are no audits to ensure humane slaughter.

Food Alliance Certified-Grassfed

Applicable to: beef, bison, lamb, goat, milk

Animals must be raised outside on pasture or range for their entire lives under this certification. GMO-based feed or any grain feeding is prohibited, and animals must only be fed grass or forage. Antibiotics are prohibited, and sick animals must be treated and can no longer be certified. There are no audits to ensure humane slaughter, and there are certain standards to reduce painful physical alterations (tail docking is permitted).

American Humane Certified

Applicable to: beef, bison, milk, pork,
turkey, chicken, eggs, duck

This certification specifies a minimum amount of space per animal to allow for natural behaviors, though animals can be confined in cages or crates and it's not required that they have access to the outdoors. The label permits the use of antibiotics to prevent diseases associated with crowded or unsanitary conditions, though no growth hormones are permitted. Painful physical alterations must be done in a manner "to minimize pain and stress," and there are no audits to ensure humane slaughter. The certification is audited by an independent third party, and annual on-farm inspections are required.

USDA Process Verified

Applicable to: beef, lamb, pork, turkey, chicken, eggs

This additional label signals that the US Department of Agriculture has verified whatever claim is promoted on the label. "By itself, the shield does not indicate anything specific about the meat product. It is meaningful only when it is used in conjunction with another claim such as 'grass fed' or 'not fed antibiotics,'" the EWG writes. The verification includes annual on-farm inspections, but there is no federal standard for any of the various label claims. Producers can write their own standards for every claim.

8.

HOW TO BUY EGGS

Oh, man, eggs are tough. The multiple claims printed on egg cartons distract from the fact that many of the claims are worthless. Most of us would like to think that the birds producing our eggs are treated humanely, but that tends to be the exception, not the rule. Eggs are less environmentally taxing than other animal proteins, but they still have an impact. Hens raised in conventional cage systems are currently the most efficient because they require less feed, which is the biggest contributor to overall environmental stress. Birds in cage-free systems require approximately 14 percent more feed.[1] This is sort of a rock-and-a-hard-place situation, since most consumers take pride in knowing the birds producing their eggs weren't confined to the worst life possible. A potential semi-solution for circumventing this mess is to get your eggs from the farmers' market, where you're more likely to access well-managed, small-scale farms where chickens serve purposes beyond producing eggs and help round out a circular model of agriculture.

When you are trying to decode those nearly illegible cartons, there are a few things to keep in mind. First, the following claims are not regulated by the FDA or the USDA, so you can pretty much ignore them:

- Farm-fresh
- Pasture-raised
- Natural/naturally raised
- Animal-friendly
- Happy hens
- No hormones (hormones are legally prohibited for use in chickens)
- Vegetarian-fed

If cartons are boasting these claims, there's a good chance the eggs come from factory farms where the hens are raised in less-than-optimal conditions.

Here is some egg terminology with a little (like a teensy bit) more weight.[2]

Caged

Caged eggs come from hens that spend most of their lives in a cage that is no bigger than a standard piece of printer paper. The animals aren't given the chance to engage in most types of normal bird behavior, like spreading their wings, standing on solid ground, or scratching.

Cage-Free

Cage-free means that the animals are not kept in cages, which is considered an improvement in living standards. Still, cage-free doesn't require hens to have outdoor access, nor does it regulate the amount of space the egg-laying hens have, so practices vary. Because the term doesn't have a legal definition, there's no guarantee that the birds can engage in natural behaviors. This claim is only useful for eggs, by the way; chickens and turkeys raised for meat are never raised in cages. Egg cartons with a US Department of Agriculture seal have a slightly extra element of proof, as this means that the agency has seen a signed affidavit stating that the hens from the producer are not raised in cages.[3]

Free-Range

Free-range is similar to cage-free, with the additional requirement of providing hens with continuous access to the outdoors during their laying cycle. The outdoor area is permitted to be fenced and covered with netlike material.

Certified Humane Pasture-Raised

Without the qualifying "certified humane," there's no guarantee with the term "pasture-raised," as it's not regulated by the FDA. When they are certified humane, pasture-raised eggs come from hens that are allotted at least 108 square feet each of outdoor area during the daytime.

There are several private, third-party certification programs (some are listed on pages 62 to 65), in which producers can voluntarily participate (usually for a fee) to further certify the environments provided for and treatments of their hens.

9.

HOW TO BUY MILK
(SO. MANY. MILKS.)

There's no simple answer to the question "What is the most sustainable milk?" By the time this book is printed, there will no doubt be a new milk on the shelf and popping up in cafés worldwide, afire with the radiance of a health halo. (The fact that Dunkin' took on oat milk in 2020 indicates that consumers' thirst for dairy alternatives persists).

Whether oat milk is more sustainable than cashew milk is more sustainable than almond milk depends on a number of variables that unfortunately aren't printed on any label. As consumers, we're eager to do the "right" thing, so it's natural to want prescriptive instructions in order to make the best purchases. It's just not that easy.

"The food system is pretty complex; it doesn't come down to one thing that is sustainable—it's a suite of things," says Urvashi Rangan, the chief scientist at Grace Communications.

Though not everyone would agree, from Rangan's perspective, almond milk doesn't necessarily beat out cow's milk every single time (and by the same token, a processed veggie burger doesn't trump one from an ethically raised cow—if you believe there's such a thing).

"It all depends—how is the cow's milk being produced? How is the alternative milk being produced? It really requires an effort in deconstructing and reconstructing what's going on," she says, noting that a regenerative soil system supporting farms free of industrial pesticides can support so-called sustainable products from animals. "When you do the right things in agriculture," Rangan says, sustainability is possible. (This is a position many who support regenerative farming share.)

She worries about the alt-milk, alt-meat, alt-everything movements, and hesitates to embrace the notion that we need to replace real food with alternative forms of it. "We are starting to create ultra-processed foods to replace fresh animal and dairy products," she says. "I think we need to not be so hasty to say that's better."

Those who oppose Rangan's stance might point to the fact that meat-based products put way more strain on the environment and our resources than do plant-based foods. The meat and dairy industries make up a major part of food production's greenhouse gas emissions, and forgoing meat and dairy entirely could cut the carbon footprint of your diet in half, according to 2014 research published in the journal *Climate Change*.[1] Simply put, "The production of animal-based foods is associated with higher greenhouse gas (GHG) emissions than plant-based foods," as the study authors write. As for milk, the numbers are pretty staggering: one cup of dairy milk produces close to three times more greenhouse gas than a cup of a plant-based alternative.[2]

So, indeed, the dairy industry creates a colossal carbon footprint.

The production of dairy products requires a lot of energy—from growing the animal feed, which uses pesticides and fertilizers (another contributor to global warming), to maintaining space for the animals, to providing water for the cows, to keeping facilities clean. There are just a ton of shifting elements that draw upon energy in order to get milk-based products from the farm to the shelf. Research from *Our World in Data*, an online science publication associated with the University of Oxford, shows that 100 grams of cheese, for example, emits a median of 8.4 kilograms of greenhouse gases, while 100 grams of nuts emits a median of −0.8 kilograms. Yes, that's a negative number. "Many nut producers are carbon negative—even after accounting for other emissions and transport," write the study authors. "This is because today, tree nuts are expanding onto cropland, removing CO_2 from the air." This doesn't let nut-centric products off the hook (we'll get into that), but it does show the vast difference between animal- and plant-based foods' impacts on the environment.

And yet. And yet. Alt-milks are no miraculous panacea. One problem we've seen with the rise of plant-based milks is the intense haste with which manufacturers pounce on a trend. The world's non-dairy milk market is anticipated to hit revenues of close to $40 billion in 2024, an increase of 14 percent over the span of six years.[3]

Whether these numbers mean anything to you is beside the point. Here's the thing to pay attention to: consumers want non-dairy options, and manufacturers want to make sure they're supplying them, and current production appears to be at a rate or through a process that's way too intense for the planet to keep up with. Or, perhaps, demand has been so persistent that manufacturers haven't had the chance (or desire, really) to figure out the safest and smartest methods to churn out these products. As a result, a purchasing decision that stems from many consumers' desires to treat the environment better has reckless but unintended environmental consequences.

An investigation by the *Guardian* published in January 2020 found that bees, which are critical players in California's industrialized almond-production process, are dying by the billions.[4] "Beekeepers attributed the high mortality rate to pesticide exposure, diseases from parasites, and habitat loss," writes Annette McGivney for the *Guardian*. "However, environmentalists and organic beekeepers maintain that the real culprit is something more systemic: America's reliance on industrial agriculture methods, especially those used by the almond industry, which demands a large-scale mechanization of one of nature's most delicate natural processes." The environmentalist position perfectly ties back to Rangan's—it's not the food itself that's necessarily problematic, but the system in which the food is produced.

Okay. If you're still reading and are like, "Blah blah blah, but what's the best non-dairy milk for the environment?" let's get into it.

Here's the short of it: there is no one alternative milk that gets first place. That said, depending on your values, some milks may outweigh others, and if you look close enough, you'll find that certain brands may provide a more responsible version of an imperfectly produced product.

Please keep these variables in mind, and take these notes with a grain of salt, drop of milk, or what have you.

As you'll notice in the chart opposite, production of almond milk has the lowest gas emissions, but requires the most water. Still, as illustrative as this graphic may be, it's not all of the information. Here's a little more about some of the most popular milks on the market, and what to look for when you're buying.

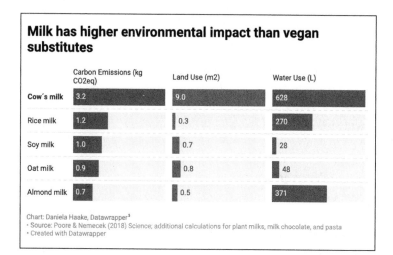

Milk has higher environmental impact than vegan substitutes

	Carbon Emissions (kg CO2eq)	Land Use (m2)	Water Use (L)
Cow´s milk	3.2	9.0	628
Rice milk	1.2	0.3	270
Soy milk	1.0	0.7	28
Oat milk	0.9	0.8	48
Almond milk	0.7	0.5	371

Chart: Daniela Haake, Datawrapper[5]
· Source: Poore & Nemecek (2018) Science; additional calculations for plant milks, milk chocolate, and pasta
· Created with Datawrapper

Soy Milk

The good: The greenhouse gases associated with soy milk's production are significantly lower than those involved in producing cow's milk. The processing of soybeans is not as water-intensive as that of other foods on this list; they use less than one-tenth of the water that almonds do.

The bad: Soybeans require more land than many other plants. Soy is often grown through monocropping, a controversial agricultural practice in which the same crop is grown repeatedly. Monocropping is associated with the depletion of soil nutrients and a dependence on fossil-fuel-backed pesticides. Soybeans are Roundup Ready, "which means they've been genetically engineered to withstand heavy doses of the herbicide glyphosate [trade name: Roundup], which pollutes ecosystems and is increasingly linked to cancer risk, especially among farmworkers," according to FoodPrint.[6] There's a really high demand for soy—beyond milk, it's used for tofu, oils, meat substitutes, animal feed, and more—and the increase in soybean agriculture has led to deforestation and the destruction of other natural habitats around the world. Tropical countries like Brazil, Argentina, and Paraguay are particularly at risk for increased emissions and deforestation related to soy production.[7]

The takeaway: Aim to buy organic to avoid major pesticides, and try to find the source of the product; soybeans sourced from the United States and Canada have smaller carbon footprints.

Almond Milk

The good: As mentioned above, the fact that almonds and other nuts grow on trees has the potential to be very beneficial for the environment. Researchers from the University of California, Davis, and UC Agriculture and Natural Resources found that 80 percent of the almonds grown in California are produced with a small carbon footprint. "Our research shows that one kilogram of California almonds typically produces less than one kilogram of CO_2-equivalent emissions," said Alissa Kendall, an associate professor in the UC Davis Department of Civil and Environmental Engineering.[8]

The bad: This is just a highlight reel, since there's been an incredible amount written about the detrimental consequences of the world's collective almond milk fever. Despite the relatively low emissions, growing almonds requires a ton of water. The majority of these nuts are grown in drought-stricken California, and the process is incredibly resource-intensive. (Even still, a serving of dairy milk requires twice as much water as that needed for a serving of almond milk.) Beyond being thirsty suckers, almonds are also greedy for land. And the bees! The little insects are critical for pollinating almond trees, but their lives are very much at stake, thanks to the pesticides used to keep the nuts coming.

The takeaway: Some experts recommend forgoing almond milk altogether, or at least making the stuff at home from organic almonds. If DIY almond milk is not in your game plan, you might try switching up your alt-milks every now and again, and choosing organic when you do buy.

Oat Milk

The good: You might say that almond milk walked so oat milk could run. After almond milk had its time in the limelight, oat milk came along and won over the taste buds of coffee drinkers, cereal lovers, and baristas alike. Sustainability-wise, oat milk has plenty of consumers convinced it's the most eco-friendly option. And it has a notable distinction: oats require considerably less water and land than both dairy and almond milk.

The bad: Since oat milk is the new girl in town, there's a lot less research on its environmental impact. As oat milk's production continues to ramp up, manufacturers will need more water and land. We can hope they'll manage to pull it off in the most sustainable ways. Recent reports have said conventional (and even some organic) oats can be contaminated by glyphosate, a pesticide that's been linked with cancer, in amounts above what is deemed safe by the Environmental Working Group.[9]

The takeaway: Go organic to mitigate the risk of glyphosate contamination. Keep your head up for new research about which brands are doing what to treat the earth nicely while giving the people what they want (creamy milk alternatives).

Rice Milk

The good: Rice milk requires less water to produce than dairy milk and requires much less land.[10]

The bad: Have you ever tasted rice milk? Okay, my personal biases notwithstanding, rice milk contributes more greenhouse gases than most other plant-based milks. Producing it also uses more than ten times more water than making soy milk.

The takeaway: Rice milk often comes sweetened and with other additives, such as canola oil and tapioca starch.[11] Check labels before throwing a container into your cart.

Cow's Milk

The good: While cow's milk is resource-intensive, there are visions for what global sustainable dairy farming could look like. According to the World Wildlife Fund, a group that's currently working with dairy industry stakeholders to build a more sustainable business model, with various innovations and technology, "dairy farmers can sustain natural nutrient cycles, build up healthy soils, store carbon and help regulate our climate, provide habitat for pollinators and wildlife, and purify water."[12] Some of the steps required to do so would include switching up feed to reduce emissions and implementing a circular system in which manure is used as fertilizer. The biggest challenge will be getting the industry on board.

The bad: Both cows themselves and their manure generate greenhouse gas emissions that impact climate change. And less than perfectly managed dairy farms are closely linked with both water pollution and soil degradation—both bad for the future of the planet. Poorly managed dairy farms also tend to have poorly treated cows, whose welfare is threatened by improper handling, poor health, and abuse. Most research indicates that plant-based milks emit fewer harmful greenhouse gases compared with dairy milk (but there's always Rangan's argument; see page 72).

The takeaway: If you're loyal to a certain brand of milk, make your desires known. Reach out—on social media or over the phone or email—and let producers know you want to know more about their practices and how they intend to make them more sustainable. Dairy from your local farmers' market is also more likely to come from a farm that has better practices for raising cows. If you can buy organic milk and dairy products, which have strict regulations imposed by the USDA, you'll be paying extra for cows that aren't treated with hormones or antibiotics and whose food is free of chemical fertilizers, pesticides, and genetically modified seeds.

10.

HOW TO BUY SEAFOOD

What even is sustainable seafood? Ryan Bigelow, the senior program manager at Seafood Watch, a nonprofit that educates consumers about sustainable seafood, puts it pretty straightforwardly: it's fish that we can continue to eat "in the future without impact to the environment or the species in question." More than one billion people around the world rely on seafood for their livelihood, so maintaining fish's future is vital.[1]

Overfishing, the practice of removing fish from a population at a rate too fast to be replenished through natural birth rates within that species, has led to the mass depletion of wild-caught fisheries, the degradation of ecosystems, the loss of jobs, and the loss of food security around the world.[2] There are, of course, many more problems connected with the mistreatment of the world below the surface of oceans, lakes, and rivers, from pollution to illegal fishing to slave labor within the fishing industry. If you eat fish, one way to make an impact is to spend your money on fish that is responsibly sourced and can be sustained for future generations. (But, hey, this is not a pass for the fishing industry. Consumers can be responsible, but we need the industry to actively work toward more sustainable practices, which some certainly are.)

So . . . what to eat?

GO HAM WITH CLAMS
(AND OTHER BIVALVES)

While there's a lot of nuance around the kinds of species we can eat without environmental consequence, a few species in particular lend themselves to being eaten with abandon. (Please don't take this in the completely literal sense.) Clams, mussels, and oysters—all bivalves and members of the invertebrate mollusk family—don't require added food or fertilizer to grow. They also make up the natural janitorial staff of the ocean, cleaning as they eat, helping to prevent algae blooms, which can be dangerous for other sea creatures. "In macroecological terms, mussels and their bivalve kin are the intestines of coastal eco-systems," writes environmental author Paul Greenberg for the Yale School of Forestry and Environmental Studies.[3] "Their filters remove organic particulate matter from the water column, particularly phyto-plankton." These species actually absorb excess nutrients that can be harmful to ecosystems.[4] Scientists are exploring how these shelled species' purification processes can help clean waterways.

There are some doubts about the promise of bivalves. While they're efficient to farm, they don't produce a big yield per harvest, Nathan Pelletier, an ecological economist and industrial ecologist, told Oceana.[5] After all, in these species, bodies are mostly com-posed of inedible shells.

Still, mussels in particular will grow virtually anywhere—and fast!—making them a breeze to harvest without depleting stocks, and profitable without compromising environmental ethics.[6]

What's really interesting about these spineless little guys is that plenty of die-hard vegans consider them fair game: without a central nervous system, it's unlikely that they feel pain. Scientist Jennifer Jacquet, who argues that clams, mussels, and oysters are the most ethical choice for seafood farming, writes that bivalves appear to be some kind of "evolutionary fluke." "This group of animals, protected by a hinged shell and largely sedentary, seems to be considerably less complex," she explained in an article for the *Guardian*.[7] "There are fewer welfare concerns about these species groups than about others, especially in captivity." Consuming these three types of shelled seafood is often equated with eating plants, not animals.[8]

As for what kind of miracle mollusks to look for, you might be surprised to know that farmed varieties are actually considered to be the greener pick in most scenarios.

Americans aren't big on eating mussels at home, but you can change that. Mussels are a versatile, veritably inexpensive, and nutritious choice that you can prepare and flavor in so many ways. They may seem intimidating, but we've all done much more frightening things!

So that was all the good news.

The futures of other types of seafood are not as promising. (If you don't want to have to do the work to figure out what species are safe to eat, maybe just stick to bivalves for now and eat more vegetables.) Seafood's environmental footprint is smaller than that of other animals, since fish don't require farmland or much care. But unsustainable practices—like overfishing, endangering marine life, paying abominable wages, degrading supply chain conditions, and creating water pollution—all add up to a flimsy future for eating fish.

"RULES" FOR SEAFOOD

In a piece for the *New York Times*, Paul Greenberg attempted to list three "simple" rules for eating seafood, noting that his rules are much clunkier than Michael Pollan's famously succinct mantra (that would be the famous "Eat food. Not too much. Mostly plants.").[9] Greenberg's recommendation for eating seafood:

1.   Eat American seafood.
2.   A much greater variety than we currently do.
3.   Mostly farmed filter feeders.

His maxim, he admits, needs some lengthier qualification. Fishermen who catch seafood in the United States and in a few other nations—including Canada, Norway, Iceland, Australia, and Namibia—best adhere to the conduct laid out by science-based fish management, though they are by no means perfect. Sticking to seafood from these countries means you're more likely to be eating seafood that was fished with sustainability in mind, though it isn't a promise.

Greenberg also promotes eating a range of seafood rather than sticking to the status quo. Shrimp, tuna, and salmon are the most consumed species of seafood in the United States, and each of these comes with its own list of environmental entanglements.[10] Branching out to include less popular species, including Atlantic porgy, Acadian redfish, and Pacific sablefish, writes Greenberg, can take some pressure off and reduce the unhealthy practices associated with the more popular species. As Bigelow puts it, "having the courage to step outside [shrimp, tuna, and salmon] and try new things" can benefit the seafood population and ease the pressure on the industries with poor labor practices.

Lastly, Greenberg references "farmed filter feeders," which is fancy terminology for seafood like mussels and oysters, since they "don't need feed because they strain their sustenance from the water."

Seafood labels are undeniably confusing. So even with these three rules in mind, it can be really tough to know what you're getting, and to know that what you're getting is sustainable. One thing you might want to become more comfortable with is simply asking. Ask the fishmonger or restaurant server where the fish was caught. Ask them if it is sustainable. They might not always know the answer or get the answer right, but asking will emphasize your desire for more transparency in seafood. Continuing to ask—despite feelings of embarrassment and discomfort—will increase the chances that those sitting at the top of the fishing industry will hear you and meet your demands for clarity.

HELPFUL SEAFOOD LABELS

There are a few labels that signal sustainability, says Ryan Bigelow. Labels from both the Marine Stewardship Council and the Aquaculture Stewardship Council "go an extra step in making sure whatever you're buying is what it says it is, and there's a certain level of sustainability associated with that," he says. The Global Aquaculture Alliance's "Best Aquaculture Practices" is an aquaculture certification program that addresses environmental, social, and animal welfare responsibility, as well as food safety.[11]

When you want even more information, you can look to resources like the Monterey Bay Aquarium Foundation's Seafood Watch app and the Environmental Defense Fund's Seafood Selector.

For some simple guidelines to follow, you might try eating fewer fish from the left column and more from the right column in the chart below.[12] (Please note that these are general guidelines that can vary quite a lot, especially from country to country. These recommendations are based on fish available in North America.)

Tends to Be Less Sustainable	Tends to Be More Sustainable
• Shrimp	• Mussels
• Bluefin Tuna	• Oysters
• Atlantic Cod	• Wild Alaskan Salmon
• Farmed Atlantic Salmon	• Wild Anchovies and Sardines
• Atlantic Salmon	• Lionfish
• Eel	• Tilapia
• Hamachi	• Striped Bass
• Swordfish	• Hake
• Wild-Caught Scallops	• Barramundi
• Orange Roughy	• Arctic Char (farmed)
	• Line-Caught Sablefish from Alaska or the Canadian Pacific
	• Mackerel (try Atlantic, not Spanish, mackerel)

11.

HOW TO NAVIGATE PACKAGE-FREE FOODS AND SHOP IN THE BULK SECTION

If you tried the waste audit (see page 7), maybe you've noticed that a lot of your trash comes from food packaging. It can be really frustrating to see cucumbers suffocated in plastic seals or rice packed in a thick plastic jug, but sometimes you've got to succumb to packaging to complete a recipe, fulfill a craving, or feed your children.

The bulk bin section of the grocery store—most consist of some mix of loose grains, nuts, and seeds—is a wonderful place to cut down on waste and spending. Here you're able to purchase the exact amount of food you need, rather than a pre-packaged portion that might be more than you want or can use before it expires. Research from the Portland State University's Food Industry Leadership Center found that organic bulk foods are 89 percent less expensive than their packaged counterparts.[1] (Be a *little* skeptical here, as the study was conducted on behalf of the Bulk Is Green council, an organization dedicated to increasing awareness around the environmental and economic benefits of bulk foods. Anecdotally speaking, I've found myself saving a really significant amount when I buy oats, rice, and quinoa from the bulk section.) The difference in price kind of makes you think about what you're paying for when you do purchase packaged foods (i.e., the packaging). The researchers produced some interesting hypotheticals that help put bulk buying in perspective:

- If coffee-drinking Americans purchased all of their coffee in bulk for one year, close to 240 million pounds of foil packaging would be saved from entering landfills.
- If Americans purchased all their almonds in bulk for one year, 72 million pounds of waste would be saved from landfills.

Whether these numbers from a 2012 study still stand true, we can assume that buying in bulk would keep some amount of packaging out of landfills. The trick is toting your bulk finds home in your own reusable bags, which isn't always as easy as it should be. Not all retailers are cool with shoppers bringing their own jars and containers to the grocery store. This seemingly defeats the purpose of buying in bulk in the first place. But you should always ask to use your own containers, and if you are denied, continue to press.

HOW TO BULK SHOP WITH YOUR OWN CONTAINER

At Bulk Barn, Canada's largest bulk retailer, customers are permitted to bring their own clean containers.[2] At this retailer, and at most bulk programs, here's how the process generally works:

1. Start with a clean vessel. You can use a cloth bag, a mason jar, a takeout container . . . the options are pretty limitless. Just make sure it's clean.

2. Weigh your empty container. This is called the "tare" of your container. Write the tare down, whether directly on your vessel or in a notebook or in your phone. If you tend to use the same refillable vessels over and over again, consider permanently marking its tare on the vessel so you can skip this step on your future bulk buys. One reason people love glass mason jars is because their weights are generally standard:

   - 32-oz mason jar = tare of 1.02 lbs
   - 16-oz mason jar = tare of 0.65 lbs
   - 8-oz mason jar = tare of 0.38 lbs

3. Fill your container with as much (or as little) package-free product as you desire.

Depending on the process of the particular store where you're shopping, you'll weigh your container again and keep note of the new weight, or just mark down the PLU (price look-up) or bin number associated with the product you're purchasing. When you check out, the cashier should subtract the tare of the container from the overall weight, charging you for the food only.

If a store doesn't have a bulk section or you can't find what you're looking for without packaging, here are a few questions to ask yourself:

Do I Really Need This Today?

Plastic in the produce section really ticks me off, and I'm personally less likely to compromise here than in other parts of the supermarket. When my grocery store only carries tomatoes in plastic clamshells, for example, I decide to forgo them for the week. I continue to live. Maybe you have your own arbitrary criteria that you can start adhering to like a new religion.

Is This the Most Sustainable Packaging Available for This Product?

Is it possible to find another brand of the product that is packaged more efficiently? When it comes to food, glass and aluminum are virtually always preferable to plastic.

Can I Buy a Larger Version to Reduce Waste?

Food packaged in snack sizes and single servings are ubiquitous, but their packaging adds up. Can you buy a larger tub of yogurt and then portion it out at home? Even if a recipe only calls for a cup of rice, can you invest in a big bag for future dishes? Can you freeze or pack away or do something with your excess in order to make a more efficient purchase?

Can I Change This?

There are other ways to reduce your packaging consumption. Most methods just revolve around asking.

At the farmers' market, it's pretty easy to flex your minimal packaging know-how. These spaces tend to be more personal and allow you to talk with the salesperson. Ask if they have any package-free options, or if you can transfer the berries you're buying into your own container so they can reuse the cardboard. Vendors might even consider taking back the containers you purchased from them at an earlier point.

When buying deli meat, bread, and cheese, ask the butcher or baker if they'll put your purchase in the container you brought from home.

CANS VERSUS GLASS VERSUS PLASTIC

Inevitably, you will buy some foods in packaging. This is just reality for now. So, while you may not always have the choice to buy your foods naked, you do have a better chance at being choosy about the *type* of packaging in which your food is sold. I asked Jeremy Walters, community relations manager at Republic Services, a waste-disposal company, what kind of containers would be the best to purchase, all things considered. Walters says that an eco-conscious consumer should "always aim to reduce first, reuse second, and, as a last line of sustainability defense, recycle."

Cans

Metals "always come out on top when put against plastic and glass," Walters says, because aluminum cans are infinitely recyclable, meaning they can be recycled endlessly without limitation. Better yet, "studies show that aluminum takes about 80 percent less energy to recycle than it takes to create the can from a virgin material," says Walters. And unlike the other materials, cans are accepted in every major curbside recycling program in the United States ("and likely the world," he adds).

Takeaway: Metal cans win, every time.

Glass

"While glass is a notable mention in the overall sustainability realm, it falls short when it comes to recycling alone," says Walters. "Glass is highly variable in terms of its acceptance in US recycling programs, and there are a number of things that influence when and where glass can be taken curbside."

Takeaway: If you're planning to upcycle a glass container, you can buy confidently.

Plastic

According to Walters, plastic containers sit below aluminum cans in this sustainability hierarchy. But, he stresses, the key word here is "containers," which connote bottles, jugs, and tubs. "These rigid plastic containers are best suited for recycling, and chances are if it has a #1 or #2 label on it, then it is accepted in curbside recycling,"

Walters says. The bigger issue with plastic packaging is the variability in the materials. There are seven different types of plastic, all of which are marked with a teensy number that's meant to tell the consumer how it should be recycled. Not all plastic can be recycled in the same way, which is really frustrating for consumers, and not all recycling programs will take the seven different kinds of plastics.

Takeaway: Stick to products that are stamped with #1 or #2, and try to avoid the rest.

The following table can help you better understand the multitudes of plastic and what kinds can be recycled.

Recycling Number	Symbol	Abbreviation	Polymer Name
1	**1** PETE	PETE or PET	Polyethylene Terephthalate
2	**2** HDPE	HDPE	High-Density Polyethylene
3	**3** PVC	PVC	Polyvinyl Chloride
4	**4** LDPE	LDPE	Low-Density Polyethylene

Uses	Repurposed to Make	Recyclable
Soda Bottles, Water Bottles, Salad Dressing Bottles, Medicine Jars, Peanut Butter Jars, Jelly Jars, Combs, Bean Bags, Rope, Tote Bags, Carpet, Fiberfill Material in Winter Clothing	Textiles, Carpets, Pillow Stuffing, Life Jackets, Storage Containers, Clothing, Boat Sails, Auto Parts, Sleeping Bags, Shoes, Luggage, Winter Coats	Yes
Milk Jugs, Juice Containers, Grocery Bags, Trash Bags, Motor Oil Containers, Shampoo and Conditioner Bottles, Soap Bottles, Detergent Containers, Bleach Containers, Toys	Plastic Crates, Lumber, Fencing	Yes
Some Tote Bags, Plumbing Pipes, Grocery Bags, Tile, Cling Film, Shoes, Gutters, Window Frames, Ducts, Sewage Pipes	Flooring, Mobile Home Skirting	Yes, but call your recycler
Cling Wrap, Sandwich Bags, Squeezable Bottles for Condiments Such as Honey and Mustard, Grocery Bags, Frozen Food Bags, Flexible Container Lids	Garbage Cans, Lumber	Yes, but call your recycler

Recycling Number	Symbol	Abbreviation	Polymer Name
5	(symbol: recycling triangle with 5, PP)	PP	Polypropylene
6	(symbol: recycling triangle with 6, PS)	PS	Polystyrene or Styrofoam
7	(symbol: recycling triangle with 7, OTHER)	N/A	Miscellaneous Plastics (Poly-carbonate, Polyactide, Acrylic, Acrylonitrile Butadiene, Styrene, Fiberglass, and Nylon)

Uses	Repurposed to Make	Recyclable
Plastic Diapers, Tupperware, Kitchenware, Margarine Tubs, Yogurt Containers, Prescription Bottles, Stadium Cups, Bottle Caps, Takeout Containers, Disposable Cups and Plates	Ice Scrapers, Rakes, Battery Cables	No
Disposable Coffee Cups, Plastic Food Boxes, Plastic Cutlery, Packing Foam, Packing Peanuts	Insulation, License Plate Frames, Rulers	No
CDs and DVDs, Baby Bottles, Large Water Bottles with Multiple-Gallon Capacity, Medical Storage Containers, Eyeglasses, Exterior Lighting Fixtures	Plastic Lumber (which is often used in outdoor decks, molding, and park benches)	Not usually; call your recycler to verify

It'll be impossible—really—to recycle all plastics perfectly, every time, and this is no fault of yours. The plastic industry is intent on putting the onus on you, the consumer, to responsibly care for materials that aren't capable of being cared for responsibly. What you can do right now is to buy fewer of these confusing materials while backing movements to flip the switch and oblige corporations to clean up their mess.

That's one major action you can take no matter your cause, whether you're passionate about plastic, animals, or food waste. Buy less, demand more.

ACKNOWLEDGMENTS

I didn't necessarily think I would ever write a book, nor did I think that my first book would be focused on garbage, but here we are. I must give thanks to the many teachers who, throughout my life, taught me to believe in the power of story. Thank you to Matthew Leaf, who gave me a notebook in the fifth grade so I could have a special place to write my poems. I believe the poem that prompted the gift was about smelly, rotting foods in a refrigerator, so maybe this all makes a lot of sense. To all my teachers, and especially Steve Shackel, Linda Sims, Lynn Kennedy, and Evelina Zarkh, thank you for doing what you do, for your patience and encouragement, and for cementing within me a love for the written word and a curiosity about the world.

Thank you to so many truly wonderful editors, colleagues, and managers, including Sarah Klein, Elizabeth Kuster, Laura Schocker, Amanda Chan, Lindsay Holmes, and Meredith Melnick, who helped me discover my beats and taught me the foundations of journalism. You served as pillars of strength when work got strange, and I wouldn't have made it here without you. I'm so grateful to Pilar Gerasimo for her unwavering mentorship and for always making time.

Thank you to Stephanie Wu, one of the best people I could ever hope to work with, for tolerating and emboldening my obsession with the weird, for putting me on the plastic-straw beat (hi, Adrian G.), and for always finding an answer to any question. To Catharine Smith—I don't think you know your impact, but it's immense—thank you for giving me so many opportunities to study and write about the environment. Thank you to Kate Lee and Mallory Farrugia for your sage advice and for being very special people during what we'll call a very special time. Thank you to all of the editors who've worked with me over the past few tumultuous years of layoffs; I've learned something from all of you and will always treasure your kindness.

Thank you so much, Anja Schmidt, for opening doors and for giving me this great gift with so much sweetness, smarts, and cool, and thank you to the rest of the outstanding team at Tiller Press and Simon & Schuster—Theresa DiMasi, Sam Ford, Kate Davids, Samantha Lubash, Patrick Sullivan, Laura Flavin, and Marlena Brown—for your impressive work and for making all of this real.

To my adorable and adoring friends, for loving me and rooting for me always, and to Suzy, my rock. To my sisters and brother, for making me feel strong and smart and loved. To my second family, especially Karen and Dave, for believing in me enthusiastically and unconditionally—thank you.

Thank you to my parents for giving me endless encouragement and so much time and space to read, write, think, wonder, and learn; with all of that, you have given me the world. Finally, to Ben (and our little dog, too): I'm so grateful for your infinite comfort, confidence, and optimism, and for the many times you selflessly ordered *my* favorite pizza on nights that I really needed it. I look forward to a lifetime of composting with you.

NOTES

INTRODUCTION

1. Hannah Ritchie, "FAQs on Plastics," Our World in Data, September 2, 2018, https://ourworldindata.org/faq-on-plastics.

Chapter 1:
ENVIRONMENTAL GUILT SYNDROME

1. Marc Daalder, "Climate Change as a Psychological Crisis," Newsroom, September 16, 2019, https://www.newsroom.co.nz/2019/09/15/807018/climate-change-as-a-psychological-crisis.

Chapter 2:
HOW TO START (BEING LESS OF A GARBAGE PERSON)

1. Kendra Cherry, "Positive Reinforcement and Operant Conditioning," Verywell Mind, November 29, 2019, https://www.verywellmind.com/what-is-positive-reinforcement-2795412.

2. "Break Free From Plastic Pollution Act of 2020," Plastic Pollution Coalition, accessed on March 1, 2020, https://www.plasticpollutioncoalition.org/break-free-from-plastic-pollution-act-summary.

3. Daniel Varghese, "A Beginner's Guide to Buying, Cooking, and Eating More and Better Vegetables in 2020," *GQ*, January 20, 2020, https://www.gq.com/story/how-to-buy-cook-eat-more-vegetables.

4. Chris Edwards and Jonna Meyhoff Fry, "Life Cycle Assessment of Supermarket Carrier Bags: A Review of the Bags Available in 2006," UK Environment Agency, February 2011, https://assets.publishing.service.gov.uk/government/uploads/system/uploads/attachment_data/file/291023/scho0711buan-e-e.pdf.

5. Tom Edgington, "Plastic or Paper: Which Bag Is Greener?" BBC News, January 28, 2019, https://www.bbc.com/news/business-47027792.

6. Shea Zukowski, *Salt, Lemons, Vinegar, and Baking Soda: Hundreds of Earth-Friendly Household Projects, Solutions, and Formulas* (New York: Metro Books, 2012).

7. Tianxi Yang, Jeffery Doherty, Bin Zhao, Amanda J. Kinchla, John M. Clark, and Lili He, "Effectiveness of Commercial and Homemade Washing Agents in Removing Pesticide Residues on and in Apples," *Journal of Agricultural and Food Chemistry* 65, no. 44 (2017): 9744–52, https://doi.org/10.1021/acs.jafc.7b03118.

Chapter 3:

GREENWASHING AND THE MYTH OF CONSUMER CHOICE

1. *Walker v. Nestle*; case 3:19-cv-00723-L-KSC, United States District Court, Southern District of California, April 19, 2019, https://www.truthinadvertising.org/wp-content/uploads/2019/05/Walker-v-Nestle-complaint.pdf.

2. "Our Progress in Tackling Child Labor," Nestlé Cocoa Plan, Accessed on February 2, 2020, https://www.nestlecocoaplan.com/tacklingchildlabor.

3. "Group Challenges Rainforest Alliance Earth-Friendly Seal of Approval," Truth in Advertising, April 20, 2015, https://www.truthinadvertising.org /group-challenges-rainforest-alliance-eco-friendly-seal-of-approval/.

4. Sarah Shemkus, "Better Bananas: Chiquita Settles Lawsuit over Green Marketing, but the Legal Battle Isn't Over," *Guardian*, December 19, 2014, https://www.theguardian.com/sustainable-business/2014/dec/19/chiquita -lawsuit-green-marketing-bananas-water-pollution.

5. Anna Kramer, "These 10 Companies Make a Lot of the Food We Buy. Here's How We Made Them Better," Oxfam, December 10, 2014, https://www .oxfamamerica.org/explore/stories/these-10-companies-make-a-lot-of -the-food-we-buy-heres-how-we-made-them-better/.

Chapter 4:

LOOK OUT FOR THESE BULLSHIT LABELS

1. Maria Steingoltz, Manny Picciola, and Rob Wilson, "Consumer Health Claims 3.0: The Next Generation of Mindful Food Consumption," LEK Consulting, October 15, 2018, https://www.lek.com/insights/ei/next -generation-mindful-food-consumption.

2. Center for Food Safety and Applied Nutrition, "Use of the Term Healthy on Food Labeling," US Food and Drug Administration, October 22, 2018, https://www.fda.gov/food/food-labeling-nutrition/use-term-healthy-food -labeling.

3. Roberto Ferdman, "The Word 'Natural' Helps Sell $40 Billion Worth of Food in the U.S. Every Year—and the Label Means Nothing," *Washington Post*, June 24, 2014, https://www.washingtonpost.com/news/wonk /wp/2014/06/24/the-word-natural-helps-sell-40-billion-worth-of-food-in -the-u-s-every-year-and-the-label-means-nothing/.

4. Label Insight, "New Survey from Label Insight Reveals Which Loosely-Regulated Marketing Claims Motivate Shoppers to Buy," Cision: PR Newswire, March 13, 2019, https://www.prnewswire.com/news-releases /new-survey-from-label-insight-reveals-which-loosely-regulated-marketing -claims-motivate-shoppers-to-buy-300811408.html.

5. "Consumers Treat Superfoods as 'Extra Insurance,'" University of Adelaide, July 21, 2016, https://www.adelaide.edu.au/news/news86383.html.

6. "Screening 'Green' Claims," Federal Trade Commission, Consumer Information, October 21, 2014, https://www.consumer.ftc.gov/blog/2014/10 /screening-green-claims.

7. "FTC Staff Warns Plastic Waste Bag Marketers That Their 'Oxodegradable' Claims May Be Deceptive," Federal Trade Commission, October 21, 2014, https://www.ftc.gov/news-events/press-releases/2014/10/ftc-staff-warns -plastic-waste-bag-marketers-their-oxodegradable.

Chapter 5:

HOW TO CUT BACK ON FOOD WASTE

1. "UN Report: One-Third of World's Food Wasted Annually, at Great Economic, Environmental Cost," United Nations, September 11, 2013, https://news.un.org/en/story/2013/09/448652.

2. "More than Half of All Food Produced in Canada Is Lost or Wasted, Report Says," CBC/Radio Canada, January 17, 2019, https://www.cbc.ca/news /canada/toronto/food-waste-report-second-harvest-1.4981728.

3. "Special Report on Climate Change, Desertification, Land Degradation, Sustainable Land Management, Food Security, and Greenhouse Gas Fluxes in Terrestrial Ecosystems," Intergovernmental Panel on Climate Change,

February 2017, https://www.ipcc.ch/site/assets/uploads/2018/07/sr2_back ground_report_final.pdf.

4. "Reduced Food Waste," Drawdown, https://www.drawdown.org/solutions /food/reduced-food-waste.

5. JoAnne Berkenkamp, Darby Hoover, and Yerina Mugica, "Food Matters: What We Waste and How We Can Expand the Amount of Food We Rescue," Natural Resources Defense Council, October 24, 2017, https://www.nrdc .org/resources/food-matters-what-we-waste-and-how-we-can-expand -amount-food-we-rescue.

6. "Ethylene in Fruits and Vegetables," UCSD Community Health, accessed on February 3, 2020, https://ucsdcommunityhealth.org/wp-content/uploads /2017/09/ethylene.pdf.

7. Victoria Lee Blackstone, "Advantages of Vermicompost," *SF Gate*, December 10, 2018, https://homeguides.sfgate.com/advantages-vermicompost -43263.html.

8. "Composting at Home," Environmental Protection Agency, November 13, 2019, https://www.epa.gov/recycle/composting-home.

9. Christine Costello, Esma Birisci, and Ronald G. McGarvey, "Food Waste in Campus Dining Operations: Inventory of Pre- and Post-Consumer Mass by Food Category, and Estimation of Embodied Greenhouse Gas Emissions," *Renewable Agriculture and Food Systems* 31, no. 3 (2016): 191–201, doi:10.1017/S1742170515000071.

10. Food Safety and Inspection Service, "Freezing and Food Safety," United States Department of Agriculture, June 15, 2013, https://www.fsis.usda .gov/wps/portal/fsis/topics/food-safety-education/get-answers/food -safety-fact-sheets/safe-food-handling/freezing-and-food-safety/CT_Index.

11. Food Safety and Inspection Service, "Food Product Dating," United States Department of Agriculture, October 2, 2019, https://www.fsis.usda.gov /wps/portal/fsis/topics/food-safety-education/get-answers/food-safety -fact-sheets/food-labeling/food-product-dating/food-product-dating.

12. Jill Lightner and Shannon Douglas, *Scraps, Peels, and Stems: Recipes and Tips for Rethinking Food Waste at Home* (Seattle: Skipstone, 2018).

Chapter 6:

HOW TO NAVIGATE THE PRODUCE AISLE

1. Hannah Ritchie, "You Want to Reduce the Carbon Footprint of Your Food? Focus on What You Eat, Not Whether Your Food Is Local," Our World in Data, January 24, 2020, https://ourworldindata.org/food -choice-vs-eating-local.

2. Shermain Hardesty, Libby O. Christensen, Erin McGuire, Gail Feenstra, Chick Ingels, Jim Muck, Julia Boorinakis-Harper, Cindy Fake, and Scott Oneto, "Economic Impact of Local Food Producers in the Sacramento Region," University of California Agriculture and Natural Resources, 2016, http://sfp.ucdavis.edu/files/238053.pdf.

3. Shahla M. Wunderlich, Charles Feldman, Shannon Kane, and Taraneh Hazhin, "Nutritional Quality of Organic, Conventional, and Seasonally Grown Broccoli Using Vitamin C as a Marker," *International Journal of Food Sciences and Nutrition* 59, no. 1 (2008): 34–45, https://doi.org /10.1080/09637480701453637.

4. Ibid.

5. Timothy D. Searchinger, Stefan Wirsenius, Tim Beringer, and Patrice Dumas, "Assessing the Efficiency of Changes in Land Use for Mitigating Climate

Change," *Nature* 564, no. 7735 (December 2018): 249–53, https://doi.org/10.1038/s41586-018-0757-z.

6. Anuradha Varanasi, "Is Organic Food Really Better for the Environment?" State of the Planet, Earth Institute, Columbia University, October 22, 2019, https://blogs.ei.columbia.edu/2019/10/22/organic-food-better-environment/.

7. Michelle Brandt, "Little Evidence of Health Benefits from Organic Foods, Stanford Study Finds," Stanford Medicine, September 3, 2012, https://med.stanford.edu/news/all-news/2012/09/little-evidence-of-health-benefits-from-organic-foods-study-finds.html.

8. "Regenerative Organic Agriculture," Rodale Institute, accessed on February 5, 2020, https://rodaleinstitute.org/why-organic/organic-basics/regenerative-organic-agriculture/.

9. FarmLore Films/Neon, *The Biggest Little Farm*, 2018.

10. "Pre-Cut Fruit and Vegetables Can Increase Salmonella Risk. Here's How," Global News, June 12, 2018, https://globalnews.ca/news/4268971/pre-cut-fruit-salmonella-risk/.

11. Suzanne Goldenberg, "Half of All US Food Produce Is Thrown Away, New Research Suggests," *Guardian*, July 13, 2016, https://www.theguardian.com/environment/2016/jul/13/us-food-waste-ugly-fruit-vegetables-perfect.

12. Sean Nealon, "How Clean Is Your Spinach?" UCR Today, University of California, Riverside, August 19, 2015, https://ucrtoday.ucr.edu/30972.

13. "Packaged Salad Can Contain High Levels of Bacteria," *Consumer Reports*, February 2, 2010, https://www.consumerreports.org/media-room/press-releases/2010/02/packaged-salad-can-contain-high-levels-of-bacteria/.

14. Trent Hamm, "Convenience Foods: What They Really Cost," Simple Dollar, March 11, 2010, https://www.thesimpledollar.com/save-money/convenience-foods-what-they-really-cost/.

15. Rebecca Smithers, "Salad Days Soon Over: Consumers Throw Away 40% of Bagged Leaves," *Guardian*, May 24, 2017, https://www.theguardian.com/environment/2017/may/24/salad-days-soon-over-consumers-throw-away-40-bagged-leaves.

Chapter 7:

HOW TO BUY MEAT

1. Melissa Clark, "The Meat-Lover's Guide to Eating Less Meat," *New York Times*, December 31, 2019, https://www.nytimes.com/2019/12/31/dining/flexitarian-eating-less-meat.html.

2. "Plant-Rich Diets," Drawdown, https://www.drawdown.org/solutions/food/plant-rich-diet.

3. Hannah Ritchie, "Food Production Is Responsible for One-Quarter of the World's Greenhouse Gas Emissions," Our World in Data, November 6, 2019, https://ourworldindata.org/food-ghg-emissions.

4. Clark, "The Meat-Lover's Guide to Eating Less Meat."

5. Hannah Ritchie, "Less Meat Is Nearly Always Better than Sustainable Meat, to Reduce Your Carbon Footprint," Our World in Data, February 4, 2020, https://ourworldindata.org/less-meat-or-sustainable-meat.

6. "UN Climate Change Annual Report: 2018," United Nations Framework Convention on Climate Change, 2019, https://unfccc.int/sites/default/files/resource/UN-Climate-Change-Annual-Report-2018.pdf.

7. "How False Advertising Lawsuits Help Animals," Animal Legal Defense Fund, accessed on February 14, 2020, https://aldf.org/article/how-false-advertising-lawsuits-help-animals/.

8. Lynne Curry, "How to Avoid Buying Fake Grass Fed Beef," *HuffPost*, July 26, 2019, https://www.huffpost.com/entry/grass-fed-beef-label-fake_l_5d309f0ce4b020cd99405605.

9. Tamar Haspel, "Is Grass-Fed Beef Really Better for You, the Animal and the Planet?" *Washington Post*, February 23, 2015, https://www.washingtonpost.com/lifestyle/food/is-grass-fed-beef-really-better-for-you-the-animal-and-the-planet/2015/02/23/92733524-b6d1-11e4-9423-f3d0a1ec335c_story.html.

10. "Meat and Poultry Labeling Terms," Food Safety and Inspection Service, United States Department of Agriculture, April 2011, https://www.fsis.usda.gov/wps/wcm/connect/e2853601-3edb-45d3-90dc-1bef17b7f277/Meat_and_Poultry_Labeling_Terms.pdf?MOD=AJPERES.

11. "Organic Livestock Requirements," United States Department of Agriculture, accessed on February 20, 2020, https://www.ams.usda.gov/sites/default/files/media/Organic%20Livestock/Requirements.pdf.

12. "Antibiotic Resistance and NARMS Surveillance," Centers for Disease Control and Prevention, November 21, 2019, https://www.cdc.gov/narms/faq.html.

13. Sang-Hee Jeong, Dae-Jin Kang, Myung-Woon Lim, Chang-Soo Kang, and Ha-Jung Sung, "Risk Assessment of Growth Hormones and Antimicrobial Residues in Meat," *Toxicological Research* 26, no. 4 (January 2010): 301–13, https://doi.org/10.5487/tr.2010.26.4.301.

14. Environmental Working Group, "Decoding Meat and Dairy Product Labels," accessed on March 2, 2020, https://www.ewg.org/research/labeldecoder/.

Chapter 8:

HOW TO BUY EGGS

1. Nina Shen Rastogi, "The Environmental Impact of Eggs," *Slate*, June 1, 2010, https://slate.com/technology/2010/06/the-environmental-impact-of-eggs.html.

2. Agricultural Marketing Service, "Questions and Answers—USDA Shell Egg Grading Service," United States Department of Agriculture, October 2015, https://www.ams.usda.gov/publications/qa-shell-eggs.

3. Environmental Working Group, "Decoding Meat and Dairy Product Labels."

Chapter 9:

HOW TO BUY MILK (SO. MANY. MILKS.)

1. Peter Scarborough, Paul N. Appleby, Anja Mizdrak, Adam D. M. Briggs, Ruth C. Travis, Kathryn E. Bradbury, and Timothy J. Key, "Dietary Greenhouse Gas Emissions of Meat-Eaters, Fish-Eaters, Vegetarians and Vegans in the UK," *Climatic Change* 125, no. 2 (July 2014): 179–92, https://doi.org/10.1007/s10584-014-1169-1.

2. Annette McGivney, "Almonds Are Out. Dairy Is a Disaster. So What Milk Should We Drink?" *Guardian*, January 29, 2020, https://www.theguardian.com/environment/2020/jan/28/what-plant-milk-should-i-drink-almond-killing-bees-aoe.

3. "The Global Non-Dairy Milk Market Is Projected to Reach Revenues of More than $38 Billion by 2024," MarketWatch, March 26, 2019, https://www.marketwatch.com/press-release/the-global-non-dairy-milk-market-is-projected-to-reach-revenues-of-more-than-38-billion-by-2024-2019-03-26.

4. Annette McGivney, "'Like Sending Bees to War': The Deadly Truth Behind Your Almond Milk Obsession," *Guardian*, January 8, 2020, https://www .theguardian.com/environment/2020/jan/07/honeybees-deaths-almonds -hives-aoe.

5. Daniela Haake, "Which Milk Has the Smallest Impact on the Planet?" *Chartable* (blog), Datawrapper, September 12, 2019, https://blog.datawrapper .de/cow-milk-and-vegan-milk-alternatives/.

6. Lisa Elaine Held, "Which Plant-Based Milk Is Best for the Environment?" FoodPrint, January 15, 2019, https://foodprint.org/blog/which-plant-based -milk-is-best-for-the-environment/.

7. "Soy," World Wildlife Fund, accessed on January 15, 2020, https://www .worldwildlife.org/industries/soy.

8. Pat Bailey, "Almonds Contribute Little to Carbon Emissions," College of Agricultural and Environmental Sciences, University of California, Davis, July 28, 2015, https://caes.ucdavis.edu/news/articles/2015/07/almonds-contribute -little-to-carbon-emissions.

9. Clara Guibourg and Helen Briggs, "Climate Change: Which Vegan Milk Is Best?" BBC News, February 22, 2019, https://www.bbc.com/news/science -environment-46654042.

10. Ibid.

11. Sandra Vijn, "How Innovation Can Help Bring Dairy Back in Balance with Nature," World Wildlife Fund, January 21, 2020, https://www.worldwildlife .org/blogs/sustainability-works/posts/how-innovation-can-help-bring -dairy-back-in-balance-with-nature.

12. Ibid.

Chapter 10:

HOW TO BUY SEAFOOD

1. "Nutrition: Global and Regional Food Consumption Patterns and Trends: Availability and Consumption of Fish," World Health Organization, July 1, 2020, https://www.who.int/nutrition/topics/3_food consumption/en/index5.html.

2. "Overfishing," World Wildlife Fund, accessed on March 1, 2020, https://www.worldwildlife.org/threats/overfishing.

3. Paul Greenberg, "How Mussel Farming Could Help to Clean Fouled Waters," Yale Environment 360, Yale School of Forestry & Environmental Studies, May 9, 2013, https://e360.yale.edu/features/how_mussel_farming _could_help_to_clean_fouled_waters.

4. Michelle Ma-Washington, "These Meats and Fish Are Worst for the Environment," Futurity, June 11, 2018, https://www.futurity.org/food-production -environmental-impact-1781632/.

5. Amy McDermott, "Eating Seafood Can Reduce Your Carbon Footprint, but Some Fish Are Better than Others," Oceana, February 1, 2018, https://oceana.org/blog/eating-seafood-can-reduce-your-carbon-footprint-some -fish-are-better-others.

6. Ryan Bradley, "Can Mussels Be the Sustainable Snack That Saves the Ocean?" *Fast Company*, July 25, 2018, https://www.fastcompany.com /90206744/at-the-catalina-sea-ranch-roping-mussels-is-the-thing.

7. Jennifer Jacquet, "Why Oysters, Mussels and Clams Could Hold the Key to More Ethical Fish Farming," *Guardian*, January 23, 2017, https://www .theguardian.com/sustainable-business/2017/jan/23/aquaculture-bivalves -oysters-factory-farming-environment.

8. Christopher Cox, "It's OK for Vegans to Eat Oysters," *Slate*, April 7, 2010, https://slate.com/human-interest/2010/04/it-s-ok-for-vegans-to-eat-oysters.html.

9. Paul Greenberg, "Three Simple Rules for Eating Seafood," *New York Times*, June 13, 2015, https://www.nytimes.com/2015/06/14/opinion/three-simple-rules-for-eating-seafood.html.

10. C. L. Illsley, "Most Popular Seafood Products in the United States," World Atlas, August 1, 2016, https://www.worldatlas.com/articles/most-popular-seafood-products-in-the-united-states.html.

11. "Best Aquaculture Practices First Aquaculture Certification Scheme to Earn GSSI Recognition," Best Aquaculture Practices Certification, October 4, 2017, https://bapcertification.org/blog/bap-first-aquaculture-certification-gssi-recognition/.

12. Mark Bittman, "How to Eat Fish and Still Save the Earth," *GQ*, January 3, 2017, https://www.gq.com/story/guide-to-eating-sustainable-fish.

Chapter 11:

HOW TO NAVIGATE PACKAGE-FREE FOODS AND SHOP IN THE BULK SECTION

1. "First-of-Its Kind U.S. Study Examines the Economical and Environmental Benefits of Buying Bulk Foods," Bulk Is Green Council, accessed on March 9, 2012, http://www.bulkisgreen.org/blog/post/Portland-St-University-releases-first-US-Bulk-Foods-Study.aspx.

2. "Reusable Container Program," Bulk Barn, accessed on March 1, 2020, https://www.bulkbarn.ca/reusable-container-program/Program-Steps.html.

INDEX

Note: Italic page numbers refer to charts.

ABOUT THE AUTHOR

Kate Bratskeir is a journalist based in New York City, where she lives with her spouse and dog. She writes about food and health, and believes in the right to food access and education for all. Her work has appeared in *HuffPost*, *Health*, *Fast Company*, and more.

NOTES

Here's a space to take notes, flag the most
important-to-you details from this book,
or list your grocery shopping essentials.

_____

_____

_____

_____

_____

_____

_____

_____

_____

_____

_____

_____

_____

Notes

Waste Audit

Date	Wasted Item	Quantity	Reason for Waste	Alternative to Waste

Waste Audit

Date	Wasted Item	Quantity	Reason for Waste	Alternative to Waste

Waste Audit

Date	Wasted Item	Quantity	Reason for Waste	Alternative to Waste

Waste Audit

Date	Wasted Item	Quantity	Reason for Waste	Alternative to Waste

Waste Audit

Date	Wasted Item	Quantity	Reason for Waste	Alternative to Waste

Waste Audit

Date	Wasted Item	Quantity	Reason for Waste	Alternative to Waste

Shopping List

Shopping List

_____   _____
_____   _____
_____   _____
_____   _____
_____   _____
_____   _____
_____   _____
_____   _____
_____   _____
_____   _____
_____   _____
_____   _____
_____   _____
_____   _____
_____   _____
_____   _____
_____   _____
_____   _____
_____   _____
_____   _____
_____   _____
_____   _____

Shopping List

Shopping List

_____	_____
_____	_____
_____	_____
_____	_____
_____	_____
_____	_____
_____	_____
_____	_____
_____	_____
_____	_____
_____	_____
_____	_____
_____	_____
_____	_____
_____	_____
_____	_____
_____	_____
_____	_____
_____	_____

Shopping List